T0370309

Beautiful One:
A Gift Within

An Expectant Mom's Inspirational Journal

"Lo, children are an heritage of the Lord
and the fruit of the womb is his reward."
Psalm 127:3

WESTBOW
PRESS
A DIVISION OF THOMAS NELSON
& ZONDERVAN

WestBow Press books may be ordered through booksellers or by contacting:

WestBow Press
A Division of Thomas Nelson & Zondervan
1663 Liberty Drive
Bloomington, IN 47403
www.westbowpress.com
1-(866) 928-1240

ISBN: 978-1-4497-7519-3 (sc)
ISBN: 978-1-4497-7520-9 (e)

Library of Congress Control Number: 2013913087

Printed in the United States of America.

WestBow Press rev. date: 10/29/2013

Beautiful One: A Gift Within

Romans 15:13: "Now the God of hope fill you with all joy and peace in believing, that ye may abound in hope, through the power of the Holy Ghost."

Beautiful One: A Gift Within

This is my wonderful journey with my beautiful baby while I was expecting, and is dedicated with love

Date:

From: _____ to: _____

Children are the most precious gift God gives us.

Contents

Introduction

Psalm 118:24: "This is the day which the Lord hath made; we will rejoice and be glad in it."

May God's glory shine on you and his perfect love overflow all your heart, mind and soul and richly bless you beyond measure with all of his wonderful promises fulfilling his divine destiny, will and purpose for you in this joyful and exciting time in your life, and as you journal through your pregnancy.

Hopes and Dreams

(Journaling guide)

Let God be your guide as you pray, feed, meditate, and honour his word daily, for he will lift you up and exalt you in due season.

As you pray believe in faith for God to reveal his divine will for your life, give you wisdom, and bless you abundantly with all his wonderful promises, for he honours his word.

This is an exciting time as you enter creative thoughts from God into your journal.

Psalm 37:4-5: "Delight thyself also in the Lord; and he shall give thee the desires of thine heart. Commit thy way unto the Lord, trust also in him, and he shall bring it to pass."

Matthew 7:7-8: "Ask, and it shall be given you; seek, and ye shall find; knock, and it shall be opened unto you:"
"For every one that asketh receiveth; and he that seeketh findeth; and to him that knocketh it shall be opened."

Mark 11:22-23: "And Jesus answering saith unto them, Have faith in God. For verily I say unto you. That whosoever shall say unto this mountain. Be thou removed, and be thou cast into the sea; and shall not doubt in his heart, but shall believe that those things which he saith shall come to pass; he shall have whatsoever he saith."

Celebrations and Special Events
(Journaling guide)

Celebration suggestions: births, baby showers, birthdays, anniversaries, weddings. holidays, reunions, dinners, etc.

Special Events suggestions: church, camping, hiking, fishing, boating, movies, sports, projects, hobbies, donating time, etc.

Beautiful One: A Gift Within

My baby's birth records

Ecclesiastes 11:5: "As thou knowest not what is the way of the spirit, nor how the bones do grow in the womb of her that is with child: even so thou knowest not the works of God who maketh all."

This inspirational journal is dedicated with love:

From parent's _____

To our precious baby _____

Year of birth: _____ month: _____ day: _____ at time: _____ .

Place: _____

Weight: _____ pounds, _____ ounces

Length: _____

Hair color: _____

Eye color: _____

Birthmarks: _____

Biblical meaning of my name: _____

Dedication: _____ : year: _____, month: _____, day: _____

Place: _____

Our family tree forever blossoming

Date:

victory

healing

Holy Spirit

anointed

prosperity

revelation

courage

shelter

mercy

forgiveness

compassion

abundant life

salvation

eternal life

My baby`s first pictures from my ultrasound and the wonderful experiences of this beautiful day:

Date:

Beautiful photos place here

victory

healing

Holy Spirit

anointed

prosperity

revelation

courage

shelter

mercy

forgiveness

compassion

abundant life

salvation

eternal life

Hopes and Dreams

Date:

_____

_____

_____

_____

_____

_____

_____

_____

_____

_____

_____

_____

_____

My Prayer

_____

_____

Habakkuk 2:2: "And the Lord answered me, and said, Write the vision, and make it plain upon tables, that he may run that readeth it."

Month One

Date:

Precious photos of my baby and me at month one

Beautiful photos place here

Daily Thoughts and Reflections

_____

_____

Gratefulness and Praise

_____

_____

My Prayer

_____

_____

Genesis 1:26: "And God said, Let us make man in our image, after our likeness: and let them have dominion over the fish of the sea, and over the fowl of the air, and over the cattle, and over all the earth, and over every creeping thing that creepeth upon the earth."

Date:

Answered Prayer

Gratefulness and Praise

_____

_____

My Prayer

_____

_____

We are loved beyond measure by God our heavenly Father and Creator, setting us apart from all creatures to fulfill his divine will and to do his good pleasure in our lives.

Genesis 22:17: "That in blessing I will bless thee, and in multiplying I will multiply thy seed as the stars of the heaven, and as the sand which is upon the sea shore; and thy seed shall possess the gate of his enemies."

Date:

Beautiful photos place here

Celebrations and Special Events

_____

_____

Gratefulness and Praise

_____

_____

My Prayer

_____

_____

When we devote ourselves to God, our children shall go forth and make a difference in the nations with God's love, power, and mercy.

Exodus 20:12: "Honour thy father and thy mother: that thy days may be long upon the land which the Lord thy God giveth thee."

Date:

Daily Thoughts and Reflections

_____

_____

Gratefulness and Praise

_____

_____

My Prayer

_____

_____

Love your parents unconditionally, as Christ loves us, forgiving each other's faults. This will allow you to receive overflowing blessings from God.

Deuteronomy 6:5: "And thou shalt love the Lord thy God with all thine heart, and with all thy soul, and with all thy might."

Date:

Daily Thoughts and Reflections

_____

_____

Gratefulness and Praise

_____

_____

My Prayer

_____

_____

With grateful hearts we come to you, God, for you give us everlasting joy and everlasting life. Hallelujah!

Deuteronomy 28:1: "And it shall come to pass, if thou shalt hearken diligently unto the voice of the Lord thy God, to observe and to do all his commandments which I command thee this day, that the Lord thy God will set thee on high above all the nations of the earth."

Date:

Daily Thoughts and Reflections

_____

_____

Gratefulness and Praise

_____

_____

My Prayer

_____

_____

The Lord promises us tremendous blessings when we follow and listen to him with undivided hearts and minds. He will lift us to higher ground.

Deuteronomy 29:29: "The secret things belong unto the Lord our God: but those things which are revealed belong unto us and to our children for ever, that we may do all the words of this law."

Date:

Daily Thoughts and Reflections

_____

_____

Gratefulness and Praise

_____

_____

My Prayer

_____

_____

The amazing promises of God's word belong to us as believers. We only have to believe and receive.

Ruth 2:12: "The Lord recompense thy work, and a full reward be given thee of the Lord God of Israel, under whose wings thou art come to trust."

Date:

Daily Thoughts and Reflections

_____

_____

Gratefulness and Praise

_____

_____

My Prayer

_____

_____

God will bless all the things we do to advance his kingdom, for he lives in us and provides everyday miracles to us.

I Samuel 1:27: "For this child I prayed; and the Lord hath given me my petition which I asked of him."

Date:

Daily Thoughts and Reflections

_____

_____

Gratefulness and Praise

_____

_____

My Prayer

_____

_____

God loves when we pray and lift others up before him. His love flows through us and never fails; it accomplishes that which pleases him.

I Samuel 2:1: "And Hannah prayed, and said, My heart rejoiceth in the Lord, mine horn is exalted in the Lord: my mouth is enlarged over mine enemies; because I rejoice in thy salvation."

Date:

Daily Thoughts and Reflections

_____

_____

Gratefulness and Praise

_____

_____

My Prayer

_____

_____

Knowing God gives us the inexpressibly joyous free gift of eternal life with him. The enemy can't defeat us, for Christ is ours.

I Samuel 2:2: "There is none holy as the Lord: for there is none beside thee: neither is there any rock like our God."

Date:

Daily Thoughts and Reflections

_____

_____

Gratefulness and Praise

_____

_____

My Prayer

_____

_____

O holy and awesome God, we desire you alone. You are our protector, and we put our trust in you.

Job 5:25: "thou shalt know also that thy seed shall be great, and thine offspring as the grass of the earth."

Date:

Daily Thoughts and Reflections

_____

_____

Gratefulness and Praise

_____

_____

My prayer

_____

_____

We anticipate and eagerly expect wonderful blessings from God, even unto the next generations.

Job 6:8: "Oh that I might have my request; and that God would grant me the thing that I long for!"

Date:

Daily Thoughts and Reflections

_____

_____

Gratefulness and Praise

_____

_____

My Prayer

_____

_____

Our heavenly Father knows what we truly desire and loves to give his children gifts.

Psalms 3:3: "But thou, O Lord, art a shield for me; my glory, and the lifter up of mine head."

Date:

Daily Thoughts and Reflections

_____

_____

Gratefulness and Praise

_____

_____

My Prayer

_____

_____

Our God protects us and beautifies our lives as we hope in him alone.

Psalm 3:8: "Salvation belongeth unto the Lord: thy blessing is upon thy people. Selah."

Date:

Daily Thoughts and Reflections

_____

_____

Gratefulness and Praise

_____

_____

My Prayer

_____

_____

From our God only comes eternal life, and that incredible, precious, and wonderful gift is to be cherished.

Psalm 4:3: "But know that the Lord hath set apart him that is godly for himself: the Lord will hear when I call unto him."

Date:

Daily Thoughts and Reflections

_____

_____

Gratefulness and Praise

_____

_____

My Prayer

_____

_____

We are that generation of godly people that will do great exploits for the kingdom of God, for he hears our prayers and is with us.

Psalm 4:8: "I will both lay me down in peace, and sleep: for thou, Lord, only makest me dwell in safety."

Date:

Daily Thoughts and Reflections

_____
_____

Gratefulness and Praise

_____
_____

My Prayer

_____
_____

We can be confident that God is on our side and that his ministering angels are watching over us.

Psalm 5:3: "My voice shalt thou hear in the morning, O Lord; in the morning will I direct my prayer unto thee, and I will look up."

Date:

Daily Thoughts and Reflections

_____
_____

Gratefulness and Praise

_____
_____

My Prayer

_____
_____

The dawn of a new day is a fresh beginning of the blessings God has given for his children.

victory

healing

Holy Spirit

anointed

prosperity

revelation

courage

shelter

mercy

forgiveness

compassion

abundant life

salvation

eternal life

Psalm 5:11: "But let all those that put their trust in thee rejoice: let them ever shout for joy, because thou defendest them: let them also that love thy name be joyful in thee."

Date:

Daily Thoughts and Reflections

_____

_____

Gratefulness and Praise

_____

_____

My Prayer

_____

_____

Yes, let us put unwavering trust in the Lord Jesus Christ, whose name is to be exalted and lifted high. In him we find our joy.

Psalm 5:12: "For thou, Lord, wilt bless the righteous; with favour wilt thou compass him as with a shield."

Date:

Daily Thoughts and Reflections

_____

_____

Gratefulness and Praise

_____

_____

My Prayer

_____

_____

Our God loves the righteous and gives abundantly beyond measure.

shelter
mercy
forgiveness
compassion
abundant life
salvation
eternal life

victory
healing
Holy Spirit
anointed
prosperity
revelation
courage

Psalm 7:8: "The Lord shall judge the people: judge me, O Lord, according to my righteousness, and according to mine integrity that is in me."

Date:

Daily Thoughts and Reflections

_____

_____

Gratefulness and Praise

_____

_____

My Prayer

_____

_____

Hold me accountable to your ways, God; correct me if necessary, for you are good to me.

Psalm 7:10: "My defence is of God, which safeth the upright in heart."

Date:

Daily Thoughts and Reflections

_____

_____

Gratefulness and Praise

_____

_____

My Prayer

_____

_____

For we can rely on our God to back us up; he is always there for his children.

Psalm 7:17: "I will praise the Lord according to his righteousness: and I will sing praise to the name of the Lord most high."

Date:

Daily Thoughts and Reflections

_____

_____

Gratefulness and Praise

_____

_____

My Prayer

_____

_____

God loves to hear his children's heartfelt praise and worship, and our hearts become one.

Psalm 8:1: "O Lord, how excellent is thy name in all the earth! Who hast set thy glory above the heavens."

Date:

Daily Thoughts and Reflections

_____

_____

Gratefulness and Praise

_____

_____

My Prayer

_____

_____

God and God alone is set on high, above all, and his presence fills everything.

Psalm 8:2: "Out of the mouths of babes and sucklings hast thou ordained strength because of thine enemies, that thou mightest still the enemy and the avenger."

Date:

Daily Thoughts and Reflections

_____

_____

Gratefulness and Praise

_____

_____

My Prayer

_____

_____

God hears the cries of his children and comforts them in their times of need.

❧

Psalm 8:3: "When I consider thy heavens, the work of thy fingers, the moon and the stars, which thou hast ordained."

Date:

Daily Thoughts and Reflections

_____

_____

Gratefulness and Praise

_____

_____

My Prayer

_____

_____

How awesome you are, God, who have created the vast universe for our enjoyment and pleasure.

Psalm 9:1: "I will praise thee, O Lord, with my whole heart; I will show forth all thy marvellous works."

Date:

Daily Thoughts and Reflections

_____

_____

Gratefulness and Praise

_____

_____

My Prayer

_____

_____

With voice of praise we will boast of you, God. You have made all of your beautiful creation for your children to enjoy.

Psalm 9:2: "I will be glad and rejoice in thee: I will sing praise to thy name O thou most High."

Date:

Daily Thoughts and Reflections

_____

_____

Gratefulness and Praise

_____

_____

My Prayer

_____

_____

You alone take us out of our troubles and set us on high, for we magnify and worship your holy name, Jesus.

Psalm 16:11: "Thou wilt show me the path of life: in thy presence is fullness of joy; at thy right hand there are pleasures forevermore."

Date:

Daily Thoughts and Reflections

_____

_____

Gratefulness and Praise

_____

_____

My Prayer

_____

_____

God, you make all things beautiful for our enjoyment; thank you for life worth living, for you are gracious to us.

Psalm 17:8: "Keep me as the apple of the eye, hide me under the shadow of thy wings."

Date:

Daily Thoughts and Reflections

_____

_____

Gratefulness and Praise

_____

_____

My Prayer

_____

_____

We know that we are very special and your prized possessions, God. Protect us and keep us always.

Psalm 19:14: "Let the words of my mouth, and the meditation of my heart, be acceptable in thy sight, O Lord, my strength, and my redeemer."

Date:

Daily Thoughts and Reflections

_____

_____

Gratefulness and Praise

_____

_____

My Prayer

_____

_____

Help me to speak only what is honorable to you, God, that it would bless the hearer, for you set me on higher ground.

Psalm 22:9: "But thou art he that took me out of the womb: thou didst make me hope when I was upon my mother's breasts."

Date:

Daily Thoughts and Reflections

_____

_____

Gratefulness and Praise

_____

_____

My Prayer

_____

_____

From the very beginning, God, you have made me and have given me a purpose for my life. I am eternally grateful to you.

Month Two

Date:

Precious photos of my baby and me at month two

Beautiful photos place here

Daily Thoughts and Reflections
_____
_____

Gratefulness and Praise
_____
_____

My Prayer
_____
_____

(left margin, top to bottom) shelter   mercy   forgiveness   compassion   abundant life   salvation   eternal life

(right margin, top to bottom) victory   healing   Holy Spirit   anointed   prosperity   revelation   courage

Psalm 22:10: "I was cast upon thee from the womb: thou art my God from my mother's belly."

Date:

Answered Prayer

_____

_____

Gratefulness and Praise

_____

_____

My Prayer

_____

_____

Children are the very best gift God gives us.

Psalm 23:6: "Surely goodness and mercy shall follow me all the days of my life: and I will dwell in the house of the Lord forever."

Date:

Beautiful photos place here

Celebrations and Special Events

_____

_____

Gratefulness and Praise

_____

_____

My Prayer

_____

_____

You have wrapped yourself around us, God, and have covered us with your blessings. We will live with you in glory.

Psalm 24:7: "Lift up your heads, O ye gates; even lift them up, ye everlasting doors; and the King of glory shall come in."

Date:

Daily Thoughts and Reflections

_____

_____

Gratefulness and Praise

_____

_____

My Prayer

_____

_____

Our God lives in us, and of this wonderful and marvelous gift we sing with great joy!

Psalm 27:6: "And now shall mine head be lifted up above mine enemies round about me: therefore will I offer in his tabernacle sacrifices of joy; I will sing, yea, I will sing praises unto the Lord."

Date:

Daily Thoughts and Reflections

_____

_____

Gratefulness and Praise

_____

_____

My Prayer

_____

_____

Life's challenges can be conquered when we praise and worship God with grateful and forgiving hearts.

Psalm 28:7: "The Lord is my strength and my shield; my heart trusted him, and I am helped: therefore my heart greatly rejoiceth; and with my song I will praise him."

Date:

Daily Thoughts and Reflections

_____

_____

Gratefulness and Praise

_____

_____

My Prayer

_____

_____

We can assuredly rely on God and thank him for the favour and kindness in our lives. Because of this, our hearts are glad and we sing in delight of him.

Psalm 32:8: "I will instruct thee and teach thee in the way which thou shalt go: I will guide thee with mine eye."

Date:

Daily Thoughts and Reflections

_____

_____

Gratefulness and Praise

_____

_____

My Prayer

_____

_____

God, you have shown me opportunities where others see nothing good. You have opened my eyes to behold the blessings before me.

❧

Psalm 37:23: "The steps of a good man are ordered by the Lord: and he delighteth in his way."

Date:

Daily Thoughts and Reflections

_____

_____

Gratefulness and Praise

_____

_____

My Prayer

_____

_____

Let us keep on doing right and honor God. For this we will be blissfully joyful.

Psalm 37:26: "He is ever merciful, and lendeth; and his seed is blessed."

Date:

Daily Thoughts and Reflections

_____

_____

Gratefulness and Praise

_____

_____

My Prayer

_____

_____

Out of a joyful and giving heart, one is able to receive God's blessings in overflowing abundance.

Psalm 45:1: "My heart is inditing a good matter: I speak of the things which I have made touching the King: my tongue is the pen of a ready writer."

Date:

Daily Thoughts and Reflections

_____

_____

Gratefulness and Praise

_____

_____

My Prayer

_____

_____

If we eagerly expect wonderful blessings from God, we shall see the heavens open and we shall praise him.

Psalm 45:2: "Thou art fairer than the children of men: grace is poured into thy lips: therefore God hath blessed thee forever."

Date:

Daily Thoughts and Reflections

_____

_____

Gratefulness and Praise

_____

_____

My Prayer

_____

_____

I will separate myself from ways and cares of this world, for God's ways are perfect in and through me.

Psalm 45:11: "So shall the king greatly desire thy beauty: for he is thy Lord; and worship thou him."

Date:

Daily Thoughts and Reflections

_____

_____

Gratefulness and Praise

_____

_____

My Prayer

_____

_____

Lord, you are beautiful, and lovely to behold. We come to you with hearts full of praise.

Psalm 45:16: "Instead of thy fathers shall be thy children, whom thou mayest make princes in all the earth."

Date:

Daily Thoughts and Reflections

_____

_____

Gratefulness and Praise

_____

_____

My Prayer

_____

_____

Our children will go on to a bright and glorious future that God has already predestined as their inheritance.

Psalm 46:4 "There is a river, the streams whereof shall make glad the city of God, the holy place of the tabernacles of the most high."

Date:

Daily Thoughts and Reflections

_____

_____

Gratefulness and Praise

_____

_____

My Prayer

_____

_____

You, O Lord, are the living water that fills our lives with overwhelming joy!

shelter

mercy

forgiveness

compassion

abundant life

salvation

eternal life

victory

healing

Holy Spirit

anointed

prosperity

revelation

courage

Psalm 57:8: "Awake up, my glory, psaltery and harp: I myself will awake early."

Date:

Daily Thoughts and Reflections

_____

_____

Gratefulness and Praise

_____

_____

My Prayer

_____

_____

I will greet you in awe, God. In each new and beautiful day you have made, shine on me, for I delight to hear the melodies and songs of heaven.

Psalm 66:1: "Make a joyful noise unto God, all ye lands: Sing forth the honour of his name: make his praise glorious."

Date:

Daily Thoughts and Reflections

_____

_____

Gratefulness and Praise

_____

_____

My Prayer

_____

_____

Let the sweet melody of our hearts and lips we praise him, for he is our song.

Psalm 86:3: "Be merciful unto me, O Lord: for I cry unto thee daily."

Date:

Daily Thoughts and Reflections

_____

_____

Gratefulness and Praise

_____

_____

My Prayer

_____

_____

Be with us, God. Wrap your arms around us, protect us, and keep us, for in you we have hope for our future.

Psalm 86:4: "Rejoice the soul of thy servant: for unto the, O Lord, do I lift up my soul."

Date:

Daily Thoughts and Reflections

_____

_____

Gratefulness and Praise

_____

_____

My Prayer

_____

_____

Though I am in despair, Lord, you will put a crown of joy on my head and brighten my countenance.

Psalm 86:5: "For thou, Lord, art good, and ready to forgive; and plenteous in mercy unto all them that call upon thee."

Date:

Daily Thoughts and Reflections

_____

_____

Grateful Hearts of Praise

_____

_____

My Prayer

_____

_____

You are a gracious and giving Father, forgetting our faults and shortcomings completely.

Psalm 86:6: "Give ear, O Lord, unto my prayer; and attend to the voice of my supplications."

Date:

Daily Thoughts and Reflections

_____

_____

Gratefulness and Praise

_____

_____

My Prayer

_____

_____

You are an awesome God, living and working through me with wisdom and might.

Psalm 86:7: "In the day of my trouble I will call upon the: for thou wilt answer me."

Date:

Daily Thoughts and Reflections

_____

_____

Gratefulness and Praise

_____

_____

My Prayer

_____

_____

I know you are a hearing God who know my needs even before I ask. You are my deliverer.

❧

Psalm 86:10: "For thou art great, and doest wondrous things: thou art God alone."

Date:

Daily Thoughts and Reflections

_____

_____

Gratefulness and Praise

_____

_____

My Prayer

_____

_____

You astonish us, God, and bring amazing gifts into the lives of your children.

shelter

mercy

forgiveness

compassion

abundant life

salvation

eternal life

victory

healing

Holy Spirit

anointed

prosperity

revelation

courage

Psalm 86:11: "Teach me thy way, O Lord; I will walk in thy truth: unite my heart to fear thy name."

Date:

Daily Thoughts and Reflections

_____

_____

Gratefulness and Praise

_____

_____

My Prayer

_____

_____

Be my guide, for I love your unfailing word, for my heart is knitted with yours, God.

Psalm 90:16: "Let thy work appear unto thy servants, and thy glory unto their children."

Date:

Daily Thoughts and Reflections

_____

_____

Gratefulness and Praise

_____

_____

My Prayer

_____

_____

Bless us, God, with your kingdom purposes, so that they will delight our children and generations to come.

Psalm 91:1: "He that dwelleth in the secret place of the most high shall abide under the shadow of the Almighty."

Date:

Daily Thoughts and Reflections

_____

_____

Gratefulness and Praise

_____

_____

My Prayer

_____

_____

Our meditations are set on you; God, and your living word, for you cover us with your majestic glory.

Psalm 94:9: "He that planted the ear, shall he not hear? He that formed the eye, shall he not see?"

Date:

Daily Thoughts and Reflections

_____

_____

Gratefulness and Praise

_____

_____

My Prayer

_____

_____

You are amazing, God. Your love envelopes us completely, for you made us in your image. We praise and glorify you.

Psalm 94:19: "In the multitude of my thoughts within me thy comforts delight my soul."

Date:

Daily Thoughts and Reflections

_____

_____

Gratefulness and Praise

_____

_____

My Prayer

_____

_____

All that is within me I give to you, God. Show me what to leave behind, for you bring me joy.

Psalm 96:1: "O sing unto the Lord a new song: sing unto the Lord, all the earth."

Date:

Daily Thoughts and Reflections

_____

_____

Gratefulness and Praise

_____

_____

My Prayer

_____

_____

A delightful song we sing to you, God, for you are highly exalted and lift us on high.

Psalm 100:3: "Know ye that the Lord he is God: it is he that hath made us, and not we ourselves; we are his people, and the sheep of his pasture."

Date:

Daily Thoughts and Reflections

_____

_____

Gratefulness and Praise

_____

_____

My Prayer

_____

_____

You are our wonderful creator God, and we love to follow you, for you have rewarded us with great and wonderful blessings.

Psalm 103:1: "Bless the Lord, O my soul: and all that is within me, bless his holy name."

Date:

Daily Thoughts and Reflections

_____

_____

Gratefulness and Praise

_____

_____

My Prayer

_____

_____

We ignite our hearts with your praises, for you are the flame that burns within us.

shelter

mercy

forgiveness

compassion

abundant life

salvation

eternal life

victory

healing

Holy Spirit

anointed

prosperity

revelation

courage

Psalm 103:2: "Bless the Lord, O my soul, and forget not all his benefits."

Date:

Daily Thoughts and Reflections

_____

_____

Gratefulness and praise

_____

_____

My Prayer

_____

_____

With you, God, are true riches, and our steps are taken with confidence.

Psalm 103:3: "Who forgiveth all thine iniquities; who healeth all thy diseases."

Date:

Daily Thoughts and Reflections

_____

_____

Gratefulness and Praise

_____

_____

My Prayer

_____

_____

He has removed all our faults and shortcomings from us and has restored us to wholeness. Of this we confess with our lips.

Psalm 103:4: "Who redeemeth thy life from destruction; who crowneth thee with loving-kindness and tender mercies."

Date:

Daily Thoughts and Reflections

_____

_____

Gratefulness and Praise

_____

_____

My Prayer

_____

_____

God, you keep us from calamity and bestow on us your perfect love and gentleness, which we freely give to others.

Month Three

Date:

Psalm 103:5: "Who satisfieth thy mouth with good things; so that thy youth is renewed like the eagle's."

Date:

Precious photos of my baby and me at month three

Beautiful photos place here

Daily Thoughts and Reflections

_____

_____

Gratefulness and Praise

_____

_____

My Prayer

_____

_____

The beautiful life-giving words that come from our lips edify others as well as us with wonderworking restorative power.

Psalm 103:17: "But the mercy of the Lord is from everlasting to everlasting upon them that fear him, and his righteousness unto his children's children."

Date:

Answered Prayer

_____

_____

Gratefulness and Praise

_____

_____

My Prayer

_____

_____

You, God, care for us and you show your favor to our children forever.

Psalm 103:18: "To such as keep his covenant, and to those that remember his commandments to do them."

Date:

Beautiful photos place here

Celebrations and Special Events

_____

_____

Gratefulness and Praise

_____

_____

My Prayer

_____

_____

God, we will remember your covenant and your Word, for it is our inheritance.

Psalm 103:19: "The Lord hath prepared his throne in the heavens; and his kingdom ruleth over all."

Date:

Daily Thoughts and Reflections

_____

_____

Gratefulness and Praise

_____

_____

My Prayer

_____

_____

Lord, may your glory shine on us. Change our lives, and govern all the nations, we pray.

Psalm 103:20: "Bless the Lord, ye his angels, that excel in strength, that do his commandments, hearkening unto the voice of his word."

Date:

Daily Thoughts and Reflections

_____

_____

Gratefulness and Praise

_____

_____

My Prayer

_____

_____

We praise you, God, for you are holy. All of heaven hears and angels rejoice at the sound of your commands.

Psalm 103:21: "Bless the Lord, all ye his hosts; ye ministers of his, that do his pleasure."

Date:

Daily Thoughts and Reflections

_____

_____

Gratefulness and Praise

_____

_____

My Prayer

_____

_____

For it is with extreme joy and zeal his ministering angels are sent forth on assignment for God's purposes to be fulfilled. They dramatically touch our lives.

Psalm 104:33: "I will sing unto the Lord as long as I live: I will sing praise to my God while I have my being."

Date:

Daily Thoughts and Reflections

_____

_____

Gratefulness and Praise

_____

_____

My Prayer

_____

_____

You make us happy, God, for our lives have become rivers of your love flowing from you, and we are blessed beyond belief.

Psalm 104:34: "My meditation of him shall be sweet: I will be glad in the Lord."

Date:

Daily Thoughts and Reflections

_____

_____

Gratefulness and Praise

_____

_____

My Prayer

_____

_____

It is very pleasant to be in your presence, God, for I love the peace of your Holy Spirit within me.

❧

Psalm 115:13: "He will bless them that fear the Lord, both small and great."

Date:

Daily Thoughts and Reflections

_____

_____

Gratefulness and Praise

_____

_____

My Prayer

_____

_____

You love us, Lord, and made each of us unique with special gifts and talents. For this we celebrate your goodness.

Psalm 115:14: "The Lord shall increase you more and more, you and your children."

Date:

Daily Thoughts and Reflections

_____

_____

Gratefulness and Praise

_____

_____

My Prayer

_____

_____

God is for us and has abundant blessings for our families, for he loves when we are united.

❧

Psalm 115:15: "Ye are blessed of the Lord which made heaven and earth."

Date:

Daily Thoughts and Reflections

_____

_____

Gratefulness and Praise

_____

_____

My Prayer

_____

_____

We have an everlasting hope that lives on the inside of us, for we have opened our hearts to our God.

victory

shelter   *healing*

mercy

Holy Spirit

forgiveness

anointed

compassion

abundant life   *prosperity*

salvation   *revelation*

eternal life   *courage*

Psalm 115: 16: "The heaven, even the heavens, are the Lord's: but the earth hath he given to the children of men."

Date:

Daily Thoughts and Reflections

_____

_____

Gratefulness and Praise

_____

_____

My Prayer

_____

_____

God has granted to our children this beautiful place, Earth that we live in and enjoy.

Psalm 118:14: "The Lord is my strength and song, and is become my salvation."

Date:

Daily Thoughts and Reflections

_____

_____

Gratefulness and Praise

_____

_____

My Prayer

_____

_____

We sing of his saving grace, and on our God we can rely, for he is our rock.

Psalm 118:17: "I shall not die, but live, and declare the works of the Lord."

Date:

Daily Thoughts and Reflections

_____

_____

Gratefulness and Praise

_____

_____

My Prayer

_____

_____

God, with you is the highway to life and newness for each wonderful day.

❧

Psalm 118:18: "The Lord has chastened me sore: but he hath not given me over unto death."

Date:

Daily Thoughts and Reflections

_____

_____

Gratefulness and Praise

_____

_____

My Prayer

_____

_____

The Lord corrects us because of his unfailing love for us, his children.

victory

healing

Holy Spirit

anointed

prosperity

revelation

courage

shelter

mercy

forgiveness

compassion

abundant life

salvation

eternal life

Psalm 118:19: "Open to me the gates of righteousness: I will go into them, and I will praise the Lord."

Date:

Daily Thoughts and Reflections

_____

_____

Gratefulness and Praise

_____

_____

My Prayer

_____

_____

Righteousness is a wonderful gift God has freely given; he has clothed us with it. Praise you!

Psalm 118:22: "The stone which the builders refused is become the head stone of the corner."

Date:

Daily Thoughts and Reflections

_____

_____

Gratefulness and Praise

_____

_____

My Prayer

_____

_____

Though you have been rejected, you are the rock and our God, on whom we build and put our trust.

Psalm 118:23: "This is the Lord's doing; it is marvelous in our eyes."

Date:

Daily Thoughts and Reflections

_____

_____

Gratefulness and Praise

_____

_____

My Prayer

_____

_____

We stand in awe of you, God. You fill our hearts with wonderful blessings to behold.

Psalm 118:24: "This is the day which the Lord has made; we will rejoice and be glad in it."

Date:

Daily Thoughts and Reflections

_____

_____

Gratefulness and Praise

_____

_____

My Prayer

_____

_____

Let us arise and thank God for the promises of each glorious new day.

Psalm 118:25: "Save now, I beseech thee, O Lord: O Lord I beseech thee, send now prosperity."

Date:

Daily Thoughts and Reflections

_____

_____

Gratefulness and Praise

_____

_____

My Prayer

_____

_____

You have changed my circumstances, God, and I honor you alone with all my heart and soul magnifying your Holy name.

Psalm 118:26: "Blessed be he that cometh in the name of the Lord: we have blessed you out of the house of the Lord."

Date:

Daily Thoughts and Reflections

_____

_____

Gratefulness and Praise

_____

_____

My Prayer

_____

_____

You come to us and change our lives with the very best. God you are awesome, and wonderful to your children.

Psalm 118:29: "O give thanks unto the Lord; for he is good: for his mercy endureth for ever."

Date:

Daily Thoughts and Reflections

_____

_____

Gratefulness and Praise

_____

_____

My Prayer

_____

_____

We will give thanks to you, God, for your unfailing love and mercy from generation to generation.

Psalm 119:1: "Blessed are the undefiled in the way, who walk in the law of the Lord."

Date:

Daily Thoughts and Reflections

_____

_____

Gratefulness and Praise

_____

_____

My Prayer

_____

_____

We will reap the reward granted to us, for we will keep and follow your laws, God.

Psalm 119:2: "Blessed are they that keep his testimonies, and that seek him with the whole heart."

Date:

Daily Thoughts and Reflections

_____

_____

Gratefulness and Praise

_____

_____

My Prayer

_____

_____

We will fulfill what you have ordained for our lives, for we will follow you, God, with all our hearts.

Psalm 119:7: "I will praise thee with uprightness of heart, when I shall have learned thy righteous judgments."

Date:

Daily Thoughts and Reflections

_____

_____

Gratefulness and Praise

_____

_____

My Prayer

_____

_____

I honor you God with all of my heart; teach me to make the right decisions for my life.

Psalm 119:18: "Open thou mine eyes, that I may behold wondrous things out of thy law."

Date:

Daily Thoughts and Reflections

_____

_____

Gratefulness and Praise

_____

_____

My Prayer

_____

_____

Reveal to us, God, your marvelous unfolding wisdom from your words of life, which you have spoken to us your children.

Psalm 119:24: "Thy testimonies also are my delight and my counselors."

Date:

Daily Thoughts and Reflections

_____

_____

Gratefulness and Praise

_____

_____

My Prayer

_____

_____

I have supreme joy in your words, for they have shown me the proper steps to take for all my circumstances.

victory

healing

Holy Spirit

anointed

prosperity

revelation

courage

shelter

mercy

forgiveness

compassion

abundant life

salvation

eternal life

Psalm 119:27: "Make me to understand the way of thy precepts: so shall I talk of thy wondrous works."

Date:

Daily Thoughts and Reflections

_____

_____

Gratefulness and Praise

_____

_____

My Prayer

_____

_____

When weighed down by life's cares, you, God, give me joy to overcome all obstacles.

❧

Psalm 119:32: "I will run the way of thy commandments, when thou shalt enlarge my heart."

Date:

Daily Thoughts and Reflections

_____

_____

Gratefulness and Praise

_____

_____

My Prayer

_____

_____

You are teaching me wonderful truths, God, and I eagerly expect great things for my life. With a growing heart of love, I hurry toward you.

victory

healing

Holy Spirit

anointed

prosperity

revelation

courage

shelter

mercy

forgiveness

compassion

abundant life

salvation

eternal life

Psalm 119:35: "Make me to go in the path of thy commandments; for therein do I delight."

Date:

Daily Thoughts and Reflections

_____

_____

Gratefulness and Praise

_____

_____

My Prayer

_____

_____

Lead me, Lord, to follow you. My heart pounds with excitement, for your ways are beautiful to me.

Psalm 119:73: "Thy hands have made me and fashioned me: give me understanding, that I may learn thy commandments."

Date:

Daily Thoughts and Reflections

_____

_____

Gratefulness and Praise

_____

_____

My Prayer

_____

_____

You have created us for your glory. Teach me and guide me that I may learn of your wonderful precepts.

Psalm 119:103: "How sweet are thy words unto my taste! Yea, sweeter than honey to my mouth!"

Date:

Daily Thoughts and Reflections

_____

_____

Gratefulness and Praise

_____

_____

My Prayer

_____

_____

I delight in all your words, God, for they satisfy me with joy, strengthening my heart.

Psalm 119:104: "Through thy precepts I get understanding: therefore I hate every false way."

Date:

Daily Thoughts and Reflections

_____

_____

Gratefulness and Praise

_____

_____

My Prayer

_____

_____

I choose your way, God, for you will not let me fail; your ways are sure and steadfast.

Psalm 119:105: "Thy word is a lamp unto my feet, and a light unto my path."

Date:

Daily Thoughts and Reflections

_____

_____

Gratefulness and Praise

_____

_____

My Prayer

_____

_____

You, God, illumine my steps and give me the right direction for my life.

Month Four

Date:

Precious photos of my baby and me at month four

Beautiful photos place here

Daily Thoughts and Reflections

_____

_____

Gratefulness and Praise

_____

_____

My Prayer

_____

_____

Psalm 119:114: "Thou art my hiding place and my shield: I hope in thy word."

Date:

Answered Prayer

_____

_____

Gratefulness and Praise

_____

_____

My Prayer

_____

_____

I love to curl up in your arms, Father God, as a little child, for I know you protect me.

Psalm 119:129: "Thy testimonies are wonderful: therefore doth my soul keep them."

Date:

Beautiful photos place here

Celebrations and Special Events

_____

_____

Gratefulness and Praise

_____

_____

My Prayer

_____

_____

We cherish your word, God, for the miracles you performed in past generations; you will perform also for us today and for generations yet to come.

Psalm 119:130: "The entrance of thy words giveth light; it giveth understanding unto the simple."

Date:

Daily Thoughts and Reflections

Gratefulness and Praise

My Prayer

You are unfathomable, God. We glean insight and revelation from your living word.

Psalm 119:162: "I rejoice at thy word, as one that findeth great spoil."

Date:

Daily Thoughts and Reflections

Gratefulness and Praise

My Prayer

There is unspeakable joy released from your word; it is to be very treasured, for it is true to us.

Psalm 119:164: "Seven times a day do I praise thee because of thy righteous judgments."

Date:

Daily Thoughts and Reflections

_____

_____

Gratefulness and Praise

_____

_____

My Prayer

_____

_____

Praising you, God, edifies my soul, and my meditations are of you.

⚜

Psalm 119:165: "Great peace have they which love thy law: and nothing shall offend them."

Date:

Daily Thoughts and Reflections

_____

_____

Gratefulness and Praise

_____

_____

My Prayer

_____

_____

You, Lord, make our hearts at ease in all situations.

Psalm 119:166: "Lord, I have hoped for thy salvation, and done thy commandments."

Date:

Daily Thoughts and Reflections

_____

_____

Gratefulness and Praise

_____

_____

My Prayer

_____

_____

We have a great future of eternal life, as promised in your words to us, O Lord.

Psalm 119:167: "My soul hath kept thy testimonies; and I love them exceedingly."

Date:

Daily Thoughts and Reflections

_____

_____

Gratefulness and Praise

_____

_____

My Prayer

_____

_____

I follow you with all my heart and soul, for you, God, are my delight.

Psalm 119:168: "I have kept thy precepts and thy testimonies: for all my ways are before thee."

Date:

Daily Thoughts and Reflections

_____

_____

Gratefulness and Praise

_____

_____

My Prayer

_____

_____

You know me, God, inside and out. You also know my future, for in you is my life.

Psalm 126:3: "The Lord hath done great things for us; whereof we are glad."

Date:

Daily Thoughts and Reflections

_____

_____

Gratefulness and Praise

_____

_____

My Prayer

_____

_____

You are the God of astonishment; and your amazing love for us.

Psalm 126:6: "He that goeth forth and weepeth, bearing precious seed, shall doubtless come again with rejoicing, bringing his sheaves with him."

Date:

Daily Thoughts and Reflections

_____

_____

Gratefulness and Praise

_____

_____

My Prayer

_____

_____

We shall harvest great joy, for you will wipe away all our tears.

Psalm 127:3: "Lo, children are an heritage of the Lord and the fruit of the womb is his reward."

Date:

Daily Thoughts and Reflections

_____

_____

Gratefulness and Praise

_____

_____

My Prayer

_____

_____

Children are the most precious of all gifts God gives us.

Psalm 127:4: "As arrows are in the hand of a mighty man; so are children of the youth."

Date:

Daily Thoughts and Reflections

_____

_____

Gratefulness and Praise

_____

_____

My Prayer

_____

_____

Great contentment will I find with the children you have given to us; they will go forth to impact nations for you, God.

Psalm 127:5: "Happy is the man that hath his quiver full of them: they shall not be ashamed, but they shall speak with the enemies in the gate."

Date:

Daily Thoughts and Reflections

_____

_____

Gratefulness and Praise

_____

_____

My Prayer

_____

_____

You bring smiles to our faces, God, for we love you for richly blessing us with children who will go on to do great works for your kingdom.

victory
shelter
healing
mercy
Holy Spirit
forgiveness
anointed
compassion
prosperity
abundant life
revelation
salvation
courage
eternal life

Psalm 132:12: "If thy children will keep my covenant and my testimonies that I shall teach them, their children shall also sit upon thy throne for evermore."

Date:

Daily Thoughts and Reflections

_____

_____

Gratefulness and Praise

_____

_____

My Prayer

_____

_____

The Lord will cause our children to rule and reign with him, for he will guide them always.

❧

Psalm 139:1: "O Lord, thou hast searched me, and known me."

Date:

Daily Thoughts and Reflections

_____

_____

Gratefulness and Praise

_____

_____

My Prayer

_____

_____

I am ever before you, my God, you are the love of my life.

victory

healing

Holy Spirit

anointed

prosperity

revelation

courage

shelter

mercy

forgiveness

compassion

abundant life

salvation

eternal life

Psalm 139:2: "Thou knowest my downsitting and my uprising, and thou understandest my thought afar off."

Date:

Daily Thoughts and Reflections

_____

_____

Gratefulness and Praise

_____

_____

My Prayer

_____

_____

You know my thoughts past, present, and future. My life is in your hands, God.

Psalm 139:3: "Thou compassest my path and my lying down, and art acquainted with all my ways."

Date:

Daily Thoughts and Reflections

_____

_____

Gratefulness and Praise

_____

_____

My Prayer

_____

_____

You are round about me, God, for your eyes are on your child.

Psalm 139:4: "For there is not a word in my tongue, but, lo, O Lord, thou knowest it altogether."

Date:

Daily Thoughts and Reflections

_____

_____

Gratefulness and Praise

_____

_____

My Prayer

_____

_____

You, God, are the one who formed our tongues and our lips that we should praise you. This brings sweet blessings.

Psalm 139:5: "Thou hast beset me behind and before, and laid thine hand upon me."

Date:

Daily Thoughts and Reflections

_____

_____

Gratefulness and Praise

_____

_____

My Prayer

_____

_____

You have been with me from the very beginning, for you are my creator. You uphold me with your gracious love.

Psalm 139:6: "Such knowledge is too wonderful for me; it is high, I cannot attain unto it."

Date:

Daily Thoughts and Reflections

_____

_____

Gratefulness and Praise

_____

_____

My Prayer

_____

_____

I cannot comprehend your divine wisdom; it is unsearchable.

Psalm 139:13: "For thou hast possessed my reins: thou hast covered me in my mother's womb."

Date:

Daily Thoughts and Reflections

_____

_____

Gratefulness and Praise

_____

_____

My Prayer

_____

_____

You are our maker, God, and your hand is upon us. Even from the beginning, you have cared for me.

Psalm 139:14: "I will praise thee; for I am fearfully and wonderfully made: marvelous are thy works; and that my soul knoweth right well."

Date:

Daily Thoughts and Reflections

_____

_____

Gratefulness and Praise

_____

_____

My Prayer

_____

_____

We respond to you, God, with our love. Thank you for creating us and the abundant, joy-filled life you have given us.

Psalm 139:15: "My substance was not hid from thee, when I was made in secret, and curiously wrought in the lowest parts of the earth."

Date:

Daily Thoughts and Reflections

_____

_____

Gratefulness and Praise

_____

_____

My Prayer

_____

_____

You artistically created me in my mother's womb and breathed your very life into me.

Psalm 139:16: "Thine eyes did see my substance, yet being unperfect; and in thy book all my members were written, which in continuance were fashioned, when as yet there was none of them."

Date:

Daily Thoughts and Reflections

_____

_____

Gratefulness and Praise

_____

_____

My Prayer

_____

_____

You, my God, have entered me in your book of life, and I know that you love me.

Psalm 139:23: "Search me, O God, and know my heart: try me, know my thoughts."

Date:

Daily Thoughts and Reflections

_____

_____

Gratefulness and Praise

_____

_____

My Prayer

_____

_____

I desire you, God. You give my soul peace. Thank you for loving me.

Psalm 144:12: "That our sons may be as plants grown up in their youth; that our daughters may be as corner stones, polished after the similitude of a palace."

Date:

Daily Thoughts and Reflections

_____

Gratefulness and Praise

_____

My Prayer

_____

We pray that our children may be established, reflecting your heavenly kingdom here on earth.

Psalm 144:15: "Happy is that people, that in such case: yea, happy is that people, whose God is the Lord."

Date:

Daily Thoughts and Reflections

_____

Gratefulness and Praise

_____

My Prayer

_____

You have made us extremely glad and joyous in you, God our king.

Psalm 147:3: "He healeth the broken in heart, and bindeth up their wounds."

Date:

Daily Thoughts and Reflections

_____

_____

Gratefulness and Praise

_____

_____

My Prayer

_____

_____

You have restored us, God, though we were dismayed. You have brightened our future with wonderful hope.

Psalm 147:13: "For he hath strengthened the bars of thy gates; he hath blessed thy children within thee."

Date:

Daily Thoughts and Reflections

_____

_____

Gratefulness and Praise

_____

_____

My Prayer

_____

_____

With our God we have become a strong fortress, and our children have inherited his promises.

Proverbs 1:5: "A wise man will hear, and will increase learning; and a man of understanding shall attain unto wise counsels."

Date:

Daily Thoughts and Reflections

_____

_____

Gratefulness and Praise

_____

_____

My Prayer

_____

_____

Our ears are attentive to what you have to say, God, for you have brought us gifts in people that bless us.

Proverbs 3:19: "The Lord by wisdom hath founded the earth; by understanding hath he established the heavens."

Date:

Daily Thoughts and Reflections

_____

_____

Gratefulness and Praise

_____

_____

My Prayer

_____

_____

You are mighty, God. We are in awe of you and praise you, Creator of all.

Proverbs 4:10: "Hear, O my son, and receive my sayings; and the years of life shall be many."

Date:

Daily Thoughts and Reflections

_____

_____

Gratefulness and Praise

_____

_____

My Prayer

_____

_____

Long lives have you promised, Lord, to those that love your living words.

Month Five

Date:

Precious photos of my baby and me at month five

Beautiful photos place here

Daily Thoughts and Reflections

_____

_____

Gratefulness and Praise

_____

_____

My Prayer

_____

_____

Proverbs 4:22: "So shall they be life unto thy soul, and grace to thy neck."

Date:

Answered Prayer

_____

_____

Gratefulness and Praise

_____

_____

My Prayer

_____

_____

Yes, a flowing river of life will spring up within us, with his hand of grace upon us.

Proverbs 5:7: "Hear me now therefore, O ye children, and depart not from the words of my mouth."

Date:

Beautiful photos place here

Celebrations and Special Events

_____

_____

Gratefulness and Praise

_____

_____

My Prayer

_____

_____

Let us not stray from his perfect and living words, for they release blessings, revealing God's plan for us and our children forevermore.

Proverbs 8:30: "Then I was by him, as one brought up with him: and I was daily his delight, rejoicing always before him."

Date:

Daily Thoughts and Reflections

_____

_____

Gratefulness and Praise

_____

_____

My Prayer

_____

_____

Yes, we are blessed, rejoicing in the Lord our God, for it is good and pleasant to our souls.

Proverbs 14:26: "In the fear of the Lord is strong confidence; and his children shall have a place of refuge."

Date:

Daily Thoughts and Reflections

_____

_____

Gratefulness and Praise

_____

_____

My Prayer

_____

_____

God protects us and our children; and his heavenly angels watch over our lives.

Proverbs 15:23: "A man hath joy by the answer of his mouth: and a word spoken in due season, how good it is!"

Date:

Daily Thoughts and Reflections

_____

_____

Gratefulness and Praise

_____

_____

My Prayer

_____

_____

Fill our mouths with your words of wisdom God that they would edify and give life to the hearer.

Proverbs 15:30: "The light of the eyes rejoiceth the heart: and a good report maketh the bones fat."

Date:

Daily Thoughts and Reflections

_____

_____

Gratefulness and Praise

_____

_____

My Prayer

_____

_____

Let us enjoy all of God's beautiful creation, for he alone is the giver of life, and we are wonderfully blessed by the one who brings good news unto all mankind.

Proverbs 16:3: "Commit thy works unto the Lord, and thy thoughts shall be established."

Date:

Daily Thoughts and Reflections

_____

_____

Gratefulness and Praise

_____

_____

My Prayer

_____

_____

Let us honor God with all we do, and our dreams and desires will come to fruition, blossoming in our lives.

Proverbs 16:20: "He that handleth a matter wisely shall find good: and whoso trusteth in the Lord, happy is he."

Date:

Daily Thoughts and Reflections

_____

_____

Gratefulness and Praise

_____

_____

My Prayer

_____

_____

Let us fully rely on our God, for wisdom and joy come from him.

victory

healing

Holy Spirit

anointed

prosperity

revelation

courage

shelter

mercy

forgiveness

compassion

abundant life

salvation

eternal life

Proverbs 16:21: "The wise in heart shall be called prudent: and the sweetness of the lips increaseth learning."

Date:

Daily Thoughts and Reflections

_____

_____

Gratefulness and Praise

_____

_____

My Prayer

_____

_____

For we have good judgment and wisdom for all matters. From our lips we sow seeds of love, bringing a rich harvest to us and to future generations.

Proverbs 16:24: "Pleasant words are as an honeycomb, sweet to the soul, and health to the bones."

Date:

Daily Thoughts and Reflections

_____

_____

Gratefulness and Praise

_____

_____

My Prayer

_____

_____

Like a beautiful melody are the soothing words we choose, for they bring life to all.

Proverbs 17:6: "Children's children are the crown of old men; and the glory of children are their fathers."

Date:

Daily Thoughts and Reflections

_____

_____

Gratefulness and Praise

_____

_____

My Prayer

_____

_____

Children are like precious jewels that adorn us, causing our hearts to rejoice.

Proverbs 17:22: "A merry heart doeth good like a medicine: but a broken spirit drieth the bones."

Date:

Daily Thoughts and Reflections

_____

_____

Gratefulness and Praise

_____

_____

My Prayer

_____

_____

Let us be grateful and joyous, giving praise to God, for he has made us fully alive in him.

Proverbs 20:7: "The just man walketh in his integrity: his children are blessed after him."

Date:

Daily Thoughts and Reflections

_____

_____

Gratefulness and Praise

_____

_____

My Prayer

_____

_____

We set a sure path for our children and future generations when we trust our God.

❧

Proverbs 22:6: "Train up a child in the way he should go: and when he is old, he will not depart from it."

Date:

Daily Thoughts and Reflections

_____

_____

Gratefulness and Praise

_____

_____

My Prayer

_____

_____

With godly instruction, our children will succeed in all they put their hands to.

victory

healing

Holy Spirit

anointed

prosperity

revelation

courage

shelter

mercy

forgiveness

compassion

abundant life

salvation

eternal life

Proverbs 23:24: "The father of the righteous shall greatly rejoice: and he that begetteth a wise child shall have joy in him."

Date:

Daily Thoughts and Reflections

_____

_____

Gratefulness and Praise

_____

_____

My Prayer

_____

_____

Let us give thanks for this beautiful child and cheerfully express our happiness out loud.

Proverbs 23:25: "Thy father and thy mother shall be glad, and she that bare thee shall rejoice."

Date:

Daily Thoughts and Reflections

_____

_____

Gratefulness and Praise

_____

_____

My Prayer

_____

_____

Inexpressible joy belongs to us for this most precious child God has blessed us with!

Proverbs 29:7: "The righteous considereth the cause of the poor: but the wicked regardeth not to know it."

Date:

Daily Thoughts and Reflections

_____

_____

Gratefulness and Praise

_____

_____

My Prayer

_____

_____

For we know God releases his love to others through us; when we give of our hearts, we are richly rewarded.

Proverbs 29:18: "Where there is no vision, the people perish: but he that keepeth the law, happy is he."

Date:

Daily Thoughts and Reflections

_____

_____

Gratefulness and Praise

_____

_____

My Prayer

_____

_____

O Lord, let me know your divine will for my life, that I may fulfill your destiny for me with joy, excitement, and passion, for you are my hope.

Ecclesiastes 11:5: "As thou knowest not what is the way of the spirit, nor how the bones do grow in the womb of her that is with child: even so thou knowest not the works of God who maketh all."

Date:

Daily Thoughts and Reflections

_____

_____

Gratefulness and Praise

_____

_____

My Prayer

_____

_____

God, you are the creator of us all, and we stand in awe and praise you.

Isaiah 9:6: "For unto us a child is born, unto us a son is given: and the government shall be upon his shoulder: and his name shall be called Wonderful, Counsellor, The mighty God, The everlasting father, The Prince of Peace."

Date:

Daily Thoughts and Reflections

_____

_____

Gratefulness and Praise

_____

_____

My Prayer

_____

_____

God, you sent your son, Jesus, who died on the cross so that we would be saved unto salvation and eternal life with you. We praise you, God.

victory

shelter

healing

mercy

Holy Spirit

forgiveness

anointed

Isaiah 26:3: "Thou wilt keep him in perfect peace, whose mind is stayed on thee: because he trusteth in thee."

Date:

Daily Thoughts and Reflections

_____

_____

Gratefulness and Praise

_____

_____

My Prayer

_____

_____

compassion

You are the great comforter, God. You put us at ease and you make all our ways pleasant. We meditate on you and your wonderful love for us.

prosperity

abundant life

Isaiah 40:5: "And the glory of the Lord shall be revealed, and all flesh shall see it together: for the mouth of the Lord hath spoken it."

Date:

Daily Thoughts and Reflections

_____

_____

salvation

Gratefulness and Praise

_____

_____

revelation

My Prayer

_____

_____

eternal life

courage

What a glorious day! For us, he is coming back. And all the people of the earth will rejoice.

Isaiah 40:8: "The grass withereth, the flower fadeth: but the word of our God shall stand forever."

Date:

Daily Thoughts and Reflections

_____

_____

Gratefulness and Praise

_____

_____

My Prayer

_____

_____

The wonderworking power of the word of God is for all generations unto eternity. Hallelujah!

Isaiah 40:10: "Behold, the Lord God will come with strong hand, and his arm shall rule for him: behold, his reward is with him, and his work before him."

Date:

Daily Thoughts and Reflections

_____

_____

Gratefulness and Praise

_____

_____

My Prayer

_____

_____

Yes, our God will rescue us and set us on high to rule and reign with him forever.

Isaiah 40:11: "He shall feed his flock like a shepherd: he shall gather the lambs with his arm, and carry them in his bosom, and he shall gently lead those that are with young."

Date:

Daily Thoughts and Reflections

_____

_____

Gratefulness and Praise

_____

_____

My Prayer

_____

_____

God does take care of people and will nurture and guide us in raising our children.

Isaiah 40:12: "Who hath measured the waters in the hollow of his hand, and meted out heaven with the span, and comprehended the dust of the earth in a measure, and weighed the mountains in scales, and the hills in a balance?"

Date:

Daily Thoughts and Reflections

_____

_____

Gratefulness and Praise

_____

_____

My Prayer

_____

_____

Our glorious God of all creation holds everything in his hands.

Isaiah 40:28: "Hast thou not known? Hast thou not heard, that the everlasting God, the Lord, the creator of the ends of the earth, fainteth not, neither is he weary? There is no searching of his understanding."

Date:

Daily Thoughts and Reflections

_____

_____

Gratefulness and Praise

_____

_____

My Prayer

_____

_____

Our God is infinite in power and might and is superior in wisdom.

Isaiah 40:31: But they that wait upon the Lord shall renew their strength; they shall mount up with wings as eagles; they shall run, and not be weary; and they shall walk, and not faint."

Date:

Daily Thoughts and Reflections

_____

_____

Gratefulness and Praise

_____

_____

My Prayer

_____

_____

God's promise to us is an invigorating zest for life, full of his strength working in and through us.

Isaiah 43:7: "Even every one that is called by my name: for I created him for my glory, I have formed him; yea, I have made him."

Date:

Daily Thoughts and Reflections

_____

_____

Gratefulness and Praise

_____

_____

My Prayer

_____

_____

We are very special in the eyes of God our maker, for he has destined us for his glory.

❧

Isaiah 44:3: "For I will pour water upon him that is thirsty, and floods upon dry ground: I will pour my spirit upon thy seed, and my blessing upon thine offspring."

Date:

Daily Thoughts and Reflections

_____

_____

Gratefulness and Praise

_____

_____

My Prayer

_____

_____

God quenches our thirst with his living water, the word. He will bring to life the deserts in our lives, giving to us his Holy Spirit and blessing us and our children.

Isaiah 44:4: "And they shall spring up as among the grass, as willows by the water courses."

Date:

Daily Thoughts and Reflections

_____

_____

Gratefulness and Praise

_____

_____

My Prayer

_____

_____

Yes and amen, our children will grow as well-watered shoots with an overflowing of abundant blessings from our God.

Isaiah 44:24: "Thus saith the Lord, thy redeemer, and he that formed thee from the womb, I am the Lord that maketh all things; that stretcheth forth the heavens alone; that spreadeth aboard the earth by myself."

Date:

Daily Thoughts and Reflections

_____

_____

Gratefulness and Praise

_____

_____

My Prayer

_____

_____

God the creator of the vast universe, the one who formed our very being, has redeemed us from the pit. We are alive in him!

Isaiah 45:3: "And I will give thee the treasures of darkness, and hidden riches of secret places, that thou mayest know that I, the Lord, which call thee by thy name, am the God of Israel."

Date:

Daily Thoughts and Reflections

_____

_____

Gratefulness and Praise

_____

_____

My Prayer

_____

_____

God surprises us with gifts he has laid up for us in heaven, and we truly know it is God who has blessed us.

Month Six

Date:

Precious photos of my baby and me at month six

Beautiful photos place here

Daily Thoughts and Reflections

_____

_____

Gratefulness and Praise

_____

_____

My Prayer

_____

_____

Isaiah 49:15: "Can a woman forget her sucking child, that she should not have compassion on the son of her womb? Yea, they may forget, yet will I not forget thee."

Date:

Answered Prayer

_____

_____

Gratefulness and Praise

_____

_____

My Prayer

_____

_____

We are always before God, for he cares for us deeply. We are his very precious children.

Isaiah 49:16: "Behold, I have graven thee upon the palms of my hands; thy walls are continually before me."

Date:

Beautiful photos place here

Celebrations and Special Events

_____

_____

Gratefulness and Praise

_____

_____

My Prayer

_____

_____

God loves us unconditionally, and we are a very special part of him.

Isaiah 51:3: "For the Lord shall comfort Zion: he will comfort all her waste places; and he will make her wilderness like Eden, and her desert like the garden of the Lord; joy and gladness shall be found therein, thanksgiving, and the voice of melody."

Date:

Daily Thoughts and Reflections

_____

_____

Gratefulness and Praise

_____

_____

My Prayer

_____

_____

O beautiful Lord, we greatly desire to come to your garden, rejoicing before you.

Isaiah 51:16: "And I have put my words in thy mouth, and I have covered thee in the shadow of mine hand, that I may plant the heavens, and lay the foundations of the earth, and say unto Zion, thou art my people."

Date:

Daily Thoughts and Reflections

_____

_____

Gratefulness and Praise

_____

_____

My Prayer

_____

_____

God, use my mouth and speak through me, for you have shown me marvelous things. I glorify you.

Isaiah 52:7: "How beautiful upon the mountains are the feet of him that bringeth good tidings, that publisheth peace; that bringeth good tidings of good, that publisheth salvation; that saith unto Zion, Thy God reigneth!"

Date:

Daily Thoughts and Reflections

_____

_____

Gratefulness and Praise

_____

_____

My Prayer

_____

_____

Praise you, Jesus, for you are lovely. We praise you for giving us hope.

Isaiah 54:13: "And all thy children shall be taught of the Lord; and great shall be the peace of thy children."

Dare;

Daily Thoughts and Reflections

_____

_____

Gratefulness and Praise

_____

_____

My Prayer

_____

_____

Our children shall be brought up loving you, God, and your living words, and we shall be blessed by you forever.

Isaiah 54:17: "No weapon that is formed against thee shall prosper; and every tongue that rise against thee in judgment thou shalt condemn. This is the heritage of the servants of the Lord, and their righteousness is of me, saith the Lord."

Date:

Daily Thoughts and Reflections

_____

_____

Gratefulness and Praise

_____

_____

My Prayer

_____

_____

You are our shield, God, and nothing shall we fear, for you have set us above the enemy and anointed us for your good pleasure.

Isaiah 55:1: "Ho, every one that thirsteth, come ye to the waters, and he that hath no money; come ye, buy, and eat; yea, come, buy wine and milk without money and without price."

Date:

Daily Thoughts and Reflections

_____

_____

Gratefulness and Praise

_____

_____

My Prayer

_____

_____

There is no cost for what God freely supplies, for he has made the payment on our behalf, because of his great and wonderful love for us.

Isaiah 55:2: "Wherefore do ye spend money for that which is not bread? And your labour for that which satisfieth not? Hearken diligently unto me, and eat ye that which is good, and let your soul delight itself in fatness."

Date:

Daily Thoughts and Reflections

_____

_____

Gratefulness and Praise

_____

_____

My Prayer

_____

_____

For you, God, will show us the way we should go, and we are content with the great blessings we have received from your word.

❧

Isaiah 55:6: "Seek ye the Lord while he may be found, call ye upon him while he is near."

Date:

Daily Thoughts and Reflections

_____

_____

Gratefulness and Praise

_____

_____

My Prayer

_____

_____

We seek you, Lord, with all our hearts, and we call on your name to save us.

Isaiah 55:9: "For my Thoughts are not your thoughts, neither are your ways my ways, saith the Lord."

Date:

Daily Thoughts and Reflections

_____

_____

Gratefulness and Praise

_____

_____

My Prayer

_____

_____

You are highly exalted, God, and you are the only one and true God, who knows what is best for us.

Isaiah 55:10: "For as the rain cometh down, and the snow from heaven, and returneth not thither, but watereth the earth, and maketh it bring forth and bud, that it may give seed to the sower, and bread to the eater."

Date:

Daily Thoughts and Reflections

_____

_____

Gratefulness and Praise

_____

_____

My Prayer

_____

_____

It is our God who abundantly supplies all our needs and satisfies us always.

Isaiah 55:11: "So shall my word be that goeth forth out of my mouth: it shall not return unto me void, but it shall accomplish that which I please, and it shall prosper in the thing whereto I sent it."

Date:

Daily Thoughts and Reflections

_____

_____

Gratefulness and Praise

_____

_____

My Prayer

_____

_____

For God's word is powerful, working in and through us, fulfilling his will for our lives.

Isaiah 55:12: "For ye shall go out with joy, and be led forth with peace: the mountains and the hills shall break forth before you into singing, and all the trees of the field shall clap their hands."

Date:

Daily Thoughts and Reflections

_____

_____

Gratefulness and Praise

_____

_____

My Prayer

_____

_____

God, all that you have made praises you joyously, for it is only you that give my soul peace.

victory

healing

Holy Spirit

anointed

prosperity

revelation

courage

shelter

mercy

forgiveness

compassion

abundant life

salvation

eternal life

Isaiah 55:13: "Instead of the thorn shall come up the fir tree, and instead of the brier shall come up the myrtle tree: and it shall be to the Lord for a name, for an everlasting sign that shall not be cut off."

Date:

Daily Thoughts and Reflections

_____

_____

Gratefulness and Praise

_____

_____

My Prayer

_____

_____

It is our God who changes our circumstances and beautifies our lives with his blessings.

Isaiah 58:10: "And if thou draw out thy soul to the hungry, and satisfy the afflicted soul; then shall thy light rise in obscurity and thy darkness be as the noonday."

Date:

Daily Thoughts and Reflections

_____

_____

Gratefulness and Praise

_____

_____

My Prayer

_____

_____

Our joy is released in our giving, and with joy and gladness we receive the blessings of abundance from the Lord.

Isaiah 58:11: "And the Lord shall guide thee continually, and satisfy thy soul in a drought, and make fat thy bones: and thou shalt be like a watered garden, and like a spring of water, whose waters fail not."

Date:

Daily Thoughts and Reflections

_____

_____

Gratefulness and Praise

_____

_____

My Prayer

_____

_____

The blessings of the Lord overflow into our lives and the lives of those we love.

Isaiah 59:21: "As for me, this is my covenant with them, saith the Lord; My spirit that is upon thee, and my words which I have put in thy mouth, shall not depart out of thy mouth, nor out of the mouth of thy seed, nor out of the mouth of thy seed's seed, saith the Lord, from henceforth and for ever."

Date:

Daily Thoughts and Reflections

_____

_____

Gratefulness and Praise

_____

_____

My Prayer

_____

_____

God's honorable word is relevant for us today and for generations to come—and unto eternity.

Jeremiah 1:5: "Before I formed thee in the belly I knew thee; and before thou camest forth out of the womb I sanctified thee, and ordained thee a prophet unto the nations."

Date:

Daily Thoughts and Reflections

_____

_____

Gratefulness and Praise

_____

_____

My Prayer

_____

_____

We were with you, God, from the very beginning, set apart and anointed by you to share your message of the gospel with the world.

Jeremiah 17:7: "Blessed is the man that trusteth in the Lord, and whose hope the Lord is. 17:8 For he shall be as a tree planted by the waters, and that spreadeth out her roots by the river, and shall not see when heat cometh, but her leaf shall be green; and shall not be careful in the year of drought, neither shall cease from yielding fruit."

Date:

Daily Thoughts and Reflections

_____

_____

Gratefulness and Praise

_____

_____

My Prayer

_____

_____

God, you are our sustenance. From you we derive all life, and our lives flourish, for you have blessed us from heaven.

Jeremiah 29:11: "For I know the thoughts that I think toward you, saith the Lord, thoughts of peace, and not of evil, to give you an expected end."

Date:

Daily Thoughts and Reflections

_____

_____

Gratefulness and Praise

_____

_____

My Prayer

_____

_____

Thank you for your love toward me and for my future hope, for you make my heart glad.

Jeremiah 29:12: "Then shall ye call upon me, and ye shall go and pray unto me, and I will hearken unto you."

Date:

Daily Thoughts and Reflections

_____

_____

Gratefulness and Praise

_____

_____

My Prayer

_____

_____

We seek you, for we adore you and long to see your face, beautiful Jesus.

Jeremiah 29:13: "And ye shall seek me, and find me, when ye shall search for me with all your heart."

Date:

Daily Thoughts and Reflections

_____

_____

Gratefulness and Praise

_____

_____

My Prayer

_____

_____

We desire to come near to you, for you cover us with your perfect love.

Zephaniah 3:17: "The Lord thy God in the midst of thee is mighty; he will save, he will rejoice over thee with joy; he will rest his love, he will joy over thee with singing."

Date:

Daily Thoughts and Reflections

_____

_____

Gratefulness and Praise

_____

_____

My Prayer

_____

_____

You are great and mighty, God. Your love is eternal, and you sing over us with songs of deliverance and joy.

Matthew 18:3: "And said, Verily I say unto you, Except ye be converted, and become as little children, ye shall not enter into the kingdom of heaven."

Date:

Daily Thoughts and Reflections

_____

_____

Gratefulness and Praise

_____

_____

My Prayer

_____

_____

With pure hearts and innocence we come to you, Father God.

Matthew 18:4: "Whosoever therefore shall humble himself as this little child, the same is greatest in the kingdom of heaven."

Date:

Daily Thoughts and Reflections

_____

_____

Gratefulness and Praise

_____

_____

My Prayer

_____

_____

Our love for you, God, is deep in our hearts, for you are our heavenly Father, who loves his children.

Matthew 18:5: "And whoso shall receive one such little child in my name receiveth me."

Date:

Daily Thoughts and Reflections

_____

_____

Gratefulness and Praise

_____

_____

My Prayer

_____

_____

God, you make all little children beautiful to bring joy into our lives.

Matthew 18:6: "But whosoever shall offend one these little ones which believe in me, it were better for him that a millstone were hanged about his neck, and that he were drowned in the depth of the sea."

Date:

Daily Thoughts and Reflections

_____

_____

Gratefulness and Praise

_____

_____

My Prayer

_____

_____

God, we pray that you put a hedge of protection around our children and keep them safe, in Jesus' name.

Matthew 18:10: "Take heed that ye despise not one of these little ones; for I say unto you, That in heaven their angels do always behold the face of my Father which is in heaven."

Date:

Daily Thoughts and Reflections

_____

_____

Gratefulness and Praise

_____

_____

My Prayer

_____

_____

God, you have blessed us with children, and we will teach them in your loving ways, for you watch over their lives.

Matthew 18:11: "For the Son of man is come to save that which was lost."

Date:

Daily Thoughts and Reflections

_____

_____

Gratefulness and Praise

_____

_____

My Prayer

_____

_____

Jesus, you have come to seek and save us and to use ordinary people like us to help spread your wonderful message of hope to all.

Matthew 18:14: "Even so it is not the will of your Father which is in heaven, that one of these little ones should perish."

Date:

Daily Thoughts and Reflections

_____
_____

Gratefulness and Praise

_____
_____

My Prayer

_____
_____

God has given a preordained purpose and a divine destiny to all his precious children.

Matthew 19:26: "But Jesus beheld them, and said unto them, With men this is impossible; but with God all things are possible."

Date:

Daily Thoughts and Reflections

_____
_____

Gratefulness and Praise

_____
_____

My Prayer

_____
_____

You have captured our hearts, and we believe in you, O awesome and wonderful God! For we have seen you perform miracles in our lives as in days past. Your word is true to us.

Mark 11:22–23: "And Jesus answering saith unto them, Have faith in God. For verily I say unto you, That whosoever shall say unto this mountain, Be thou removed , and be thou cast into the sea; and shall not doubt in his heart, but shall believe that those things which he saith shall come to pass; he shall have whatsoever he saith."

Date:

Daily Thoughts and Reflections

_____

_____

Gratefulness and Praise

_____

_____

My Prayer

_____

_____

Yes, we have complete faith in you, God, and in your wonderful promises to us, your children. We truly believe, and we speak of abundant blessings flowing into our lives and of being a blessing to others.

Month Seven

Date:

Precious photos of my baby and me at month seven

Beautiful photos place here

Daily Thoughts and Reflections

_____

_____

Gratefulness and Praise

_____

_____

My Prayer

_____

_____

Mark 11:24: "Therefore I say unto you, What things soever ye desire, when ye pray, believe that ye receive them, and ye shall have them."

Date:

Answered Prayer

_____

_____

Gratefulness and Praise

_____

_____

My Prayer

_____

_____

God, you love to give your children their heart's desires. And we know that when we pray you hear us, for this is your wonderful promise to us.

Mark 11:25: "And when ye stand praying, forgive, if ye have aught against any; that your Father also which is in heaven may forgive you your trespasses."

Date:

Beautiful photos place here

Celebrations and Special Events

_____

_____

Gratefulness and Praise

_____

_____

My Prayer

_____

_____

We are able to receive when we soften our hearts and forgive. By doing so, we remove the stumbling blocks and are able to run with joy, receiving the wonderful blessings of God.

Luke 2:10–11: "And the angel said unto them, Fear not: for, behold, I bring you good tidings of great joy, which shall be to all people.For unto you is born this day in the city of David a Saviour, which is Christ the Lord."

Date:

Daily Thoughts and Reflections

_____

_____

Gratefulness and Praise

_____

_____

My Prayer

_____

_____

Jesus came from heaven to earth as a baby to seek and save the lost that they would have eternal life.

Luke 2:12: "And this shall be a sign unto you; Ye shall find the babe wrapped in swaddling clothes, lying in a manger."

Date:

Daily Thoughts and Reflections

_____

_____

Gratefulness and Praise

_____

_____

My Prayer

_____

_____

All people would know the love of God; he sent his one and only precious child that we would come to the saving knowledge of his grace and salvation.

Luke 2:13–14: "And suddenly there was with the angel a multitude of heavenly host praising God, and saying, Glory to God in the highest, and on earth peace, good will toward men."

Date:

Daily Thoughts and Reflections

_____

_____

Gratefulness and Praise

_____

_____

My Prayer

_____

_____

All of heaven rejoices, for the Prince of Peace is with us.

John 4:14: "But whosoever drinketh of the water that I shall give him shall never thirst; but the water that I shall give him shall be in him a well of water springing up into everlasting life."

Date:

Daily Thoughts and Reflections

_____

_____

Gratefulness and Praise

_____

_____

My Prayer

_____

_____

O God, we praise you for your promise of salvation, for we believe your living words.

John 4:24: "God is a spirit: and they that worship him must worship him in spirit and in truth."

Date:

Daily Thoughts and Reflections

_____

_____

Gratefulness and Praise

_____

_____

My Prayer

_____

_____

In total abandonment, we yield our lives to you, God, and give you the highest honor and praise.

John 6:33: "For the bread of God is he which cometh down from heaven, and giveth life unto the world."

Date:

Daily Thoughts and Reflections

_____

_____

Gratefulness and Praise

_____

_____

My prayer

_____

_____

Jesus, you came to earth, died on the cross for our sins, and rose again from death on the third day that we may truly live the beautiful life that is freely given by you.

John 6:40: "And this is the will of him that sent me, that everyone which seeeth the Son, and believeth on him, may have everlasting life: and I will raise him up at the last day."

Date:

Daily Thoughts and Reflections

_____

_____

Gratefulness and Praise

_____

_____

My Prayer

_____

_____

For we have this great hope: that you, God, will rescue us, for we believe on you for our salvation.

John 7:38: "He that believeth on me, as the scripture hath said, out of his belly shall flow rivers of living water."

Date:

Daily Thoughts and Reflections

_____

_____

Gratefulness and Praise

_____

_____

My Prayer

_____

_____

We are bursting at the seams in the abundance of this precious life that you have given us, God. With great joy, we will share it with the world.

John 14:12: "Verily, verily, I say unto you. He that believeth on me, the works that I do shall he do also, and greater works than these shall he do; because I go unto my Father."

Date:

Daily Thoughts and Reflections

_____

_____

Gratefulness and Praise

_____

_____

My Prayer

_____

_____

God, you have equipped us with wonderworking power and might, that we and our children and generations to come will do mighty and marvelous miracles for your kingdom.

John 14:13–14: "And whatsoever ye shall ask in my name, that will I do, that the Father may be glorified in the Son. If ye shall ask any thing in my name, I will do it."

Date:

Daily Thoughts and Reflections

_____

_____

Gratefulness and Praise

_____

_____

My Prayer

_____

_____

All of our hopes and desires are in you, God, and you love to give your children wonderful gifts when we pray in the name of Jesus.

John 14:15: "If ye love me, keep my commandments."

Date:

Daily Thoughts and Reflections

_____

_____

Gratefulness and Praise

_____

_____

My Prayer

_____

_____

We love you, God, and find great delight in keeping your commandments.

John 14:16–17: "And I will pray the Father, and he shall give you another Comforter, that he may abide with you forever. Even the Spirit of truth; whom the world cannot receive, because it seeth him not, neither knoweth him: but ye know him; for he dwelleth with you, and shall be in you."

Date:

Daily Thoughts and Reflections

_____

_____

Gratefulness and Praise

_____

_____

My Prayer

_____

_____

Praise you, God, for giving to us your Holy Spirit.

Acts 2:17: "And it shall come to pass in the last days, saith God, I will pour out of my Spirit upon all flesh: and your sons and your daughters shall prophesy, and your young men shall see visions, and your old men shall dream dreams."

Date:

Daily Thoughts and Reflections

_____

_____

Gratefulness and Praise

_____

_____

My Prayer

_____

_____

God, you amaze us with the unfolding of your word. We pray that revelation knowledge would be released in our lives, in Jesus' name. Amen

Acts 2:26: "Therefore did my heart rejoice, and my tongue was glad; moreover also my flesh shall rest in hope."

Date:

Daily Thoughts and Reflections

_____

_____

Gratefulness and Praise

_____

_____

My Prayer

_____

_____

God, you have given me joy and refreshed me with your spirit, and my soul is at peace within me.

Acts 2:28: "Thou hast made known to me the ways of life; thou shalt make me full of joy with thy countenance."

Date:

Daily Thoughts and Reflections

_____

_____

Gratefulness and Praise

_____

_____

My Prayer

_____

_____

All your ways are pleasant and sweet to our souls, and we rejoice for your glory is upon us.

I Corinthians 6:19: "What? Know ye not that your body is the temple of the Holy Ghost which is in you, which ye have of God, and ye are not your own?"

Date:

Daily Thoughts and Reflections

_____

_____

Gratefulness and Praise

_____

_____

My Prayer

_____

_____

We honor your Holy Spirit that lives in us and shows us all truths to bless our lives.

I Corinthians 6:20: "For ye are bought with a price: therefore glorify God in your body, and in your spirit, which are God's."

Date:

Daily Thoughts and Reflections

_____

_____

Gratefulness and Praise

_____

_____

My Prayer

_____

_____

Praise you, God, for creating me and for this precious baby in my womb. We give you all the glory!

Galatians 4:7: "Wherefore thou art no more a servant, but a son; and if a son, then an heir of God through Christ."

Date:

Daily Thoughts and Reflections

_____

_____

Gratefulness and Praise

_____

_____

My Prayer

_____

_____

You have made us free by breaking our chains to the ways of this world. Now we belong to you, Father God.

Love joy peace hope faith grace favour

Galatians 6:7: "Be not deceived; God is not mocked: for whatsoever a man soweth, that shall he also reap."

Date:

Daily Thoughts and Reflections

_____

_____

Gratefulness and Praise

_____

_____

My Prayer

_____

_____

Our lives will flourish and prosper, for we sow the seeds of love. And love always succeeds.

Ephesians 1:2: "Grace be to you, and peace, from God our Father, and from the Lord Jesus Christ."

Date:

Daily Thoughts and Reflections

_____

_____

Gratefulness and Praise

_____

_____

My Prayer

_____

_____

You have covered us with your matchless grace and your peace that comforts, and you love us, God.

Ephesians 1:3: "Blessed be the God and Father of our Lord Jesus Christ, who hath blessed us with all spiritual blessings in heavenly places in Christ."

Date:

Daily Thoughts and Reflections

_____

_____

Gratefulness and Praise

_____

_____

My Prayer

_____

_____

In Christ, we have been gifted and fully supplied with all of God's attributes.

Ephesians 1:17: "That the God of our Lord Jesus Christ, the Father of glory, may give unto you the spirit of wisdom and revelation in the knowledge of him."

Date:

Daily Thoughts and Reflections

_____

_____

Gratefulness and Praise

_____

_____

My Prayer

_____

_____

We worship you and rejoice, for you generously give to your children when we pray.

Ephesians 1:18: "The eyes of your understanding being enlightened; that ye may know what is the hope of his calling, and what the riches of the glory of his inheritance in the saints."

Date:

Daily Thoughts and Reflections

_____

_____

Gratefulness and Praise

_____

_____

My Prayer

_____

_____

Reveal to me your will for my life, God, for it is my destiny and supreme joy.

Ephesians 1:19: "And what is the exceeding greatness of his power to us-ward who believe, according to the working of his mighty power."

Date:

Daily Thoughts and Reflections

_____

_____

Gratefulness and Praise

_____

_____

My Prayer

_____

_____

God, we humble ourselves before you, for you have your Holy Spirit living in us and you perform miracles through us.

Ephesians 1:20: "Which he wrought in Christ, when he raised him from the dead, and set him at his own right hand in the heavenly places."

Date:

Daily Thoughts and Reflections

_____

_____

Gratefulness and Praise

_____

_____

My Prayer

_____

_____

You give us great hope, God, for you are the only one that gives life. And we will live with you forever in your heavenly kingdom.

Ephesians 2:4–5: "But God who is rich in mercy, for his great love wherewith he loved us, Even when we were dead in sins, hath quickened us together with Christ, (by grace ye are saved)."

Date:

Daily Thoughts and Reflections

_____

_____

Gratefulness and Praise

_____

_____

My Prayer

_____

_____

God covers and wraps himself around us with his wonderful love and saving grace.

Ephesians 2:7: "That in the ages to come he might show the exceeding riches of his grace in his kindness toward us through Christ Jesus."

Date:

Daily Thoughts and Reflections

_____

_____

Gratefulness and Praise

_____

_____

My Prayer

_____

_____

We praise you, God, for loving us with your grace and tenderness, for it shall comfort our hearts and our souls.

Ephesians 2:8: "For by grace are ye saved through faith; and that not of yourselves: it is the gift of God."

Date:

Daily Thoughts and Reflections

_____

_____

Gratefulness and Praise

_____

_____

My Prayer

_____

_____

O beautiful Jesus, we love and adore you, for your grace you have freely given to us for eternal life.

victory

shelter

healing

mercy

Holy Spirit

forgiveness

Ephesians 2:10: "For we are his workmanship, created in Christ Jesus unto good works, which God hath before ordained that we should walk in them."

Date:

Daily Thoughts and Reflections

_____

_____

Gratefulness and Praise

_____

_____

My Prayer

_____

_____

compassion

anointed

With zeal and passion for you, God, we pursue our destiny, for we have a divine purpose to fulfill in this exciting life.

prosperity

abundant life

Ephesians 2:14: "For he is our peace, who hath made both one, and hath broken down the middle wall of partition between us."

Date:

Daily Thoughts and Reflections

_____

_____

Gratefulness and Praise

_____

_____

My Prayer

_____

_____

salvation

revelation

eternal life

courage

We are united with you, God, and any peace we have comes from you alone.

Ephesians 3:9: "And to make all men see what is the fellowship of the mystery, which from the beginning of the world hath been hid in God, who created all things by Jesus Christ."

Date:

Daily Thoughts and Reflections

_____

_____

Gratefulness and Praise

_____

_____

My Prayer

_____

_____

We thank and praise you, God, for revealing yourself to us and for abiding with us, your children.

Month Eight

Date:

Precious photos of my baby and me at month eight

Beautiful photos place here

Daily Thoughts and Reflections

_____

_____

Gratefulness and Praise

_____

_____

My Prayer

_____

_____

Ephesians 3:10: "To the intent that now unto the principalities and powers in heavenly places might be known by the church the manifold wisdom of God."

Date:

Answered Pray

_____

_____

Gratefulness and Praise

_____

_____

My Prayer

_____

_____

Thank you, God, for your wisdom that you reveal to us, for your love for us is eternal.

Ephesians 3:12: "In whom we have boldness and access with confidence by faith of him."

Date:

Beautiful photos place here

Celebrations and Special Events

_____

_____

Gratefulness and Praise

_____

_____

My Prayer

_____

_____

We know we can always come to you, heavenly Father, for you love us, your precious children.

Ephesians 3:16: "That he would grant you, according to the riches of his glory, to be strengthened with might by his Spirit in the inner man."

Date:

Daily Thoughts and Reflections

_____

_____

Gratefulness and Praise

_____

_____

My Prayer

_____

_____

God, you strengthen me daily with your supernatural power.

Ephesians 3:17: "That Christ may dwell in your hearts by faith; that ye, being rooted and grounded in love."

Date:

Daily Thoughts and Reflections

_____

_____

Gratefulness and Praise

_____

_____

My Prayer

_____

_____

We open our hearts to you, O God, for the fragrance of your love is a sweet perfume.

Ephesians 3:19: "And to know the love of Christ, which passeth knowledge, that ye might be filled with all the fullness of God."

Date:

Daily Thoughts and Reflections

_____

_____

Gratefulness and Praise

_____

_____

My Prayer

_____

_____

Our gaze is on you, God, for you are our heart's desire. We worship and adore you, the lover of our souls.

Ephesians 3:20: "Now unto him that is able to do exceeding abundantly above all that we ask or think, according to the power that worketh in us."

Date:

Daily Thoughts and Reflections

_____

_____

Gratefulness and Praise

_____

_____

My Prayer

_____

_____

Your miracle-working power flows through me, for I abandon my heart to you, my God.

Ephesians 3:21: "Unto him be glory in the church by Christ Jesus throughout all ages, world without end. Amen."

Date:

Daily Thoughts and Reflections

_____

_____

Gratefulness and Praise

_____

_____

My Prayer

_____

_____

We exalt you, Lord Jesus, and praise and magnify your glorious name.

❧

Ephesians 4:32: "And be ye kind one to another, tenderhearted, forgiving one another, even as God for Christ's sake hath forgiven you."

Date:

Daily Thoughts and Reflections

_____

_____

Gratefulness and Praise

_____

_____

My Prayer

_____

_____

Let us sow the seeds of kindness and tender-heartedness, for we will reap a rich harvest.

victory

shelter

healing

mercy

Holy Spirit

forgiveness

anointed

compassion

prosperity

abundant life

revelation

salvation

eternal life

courage

Ephesians 5:1: "Be ye therefore followers of God, as dear children."

Date:

Daily Thoughts and Reflections

_____

_____

Gratefulness and Praise

_____

_____

My Prayer

_____

_____

We love to follow you, God, for you make our ways joyous.

Ephesians 5:2: "And walk in love, as Christ also hath loved us, and hath given himself for us an offering and a sacrifice to God for a sweetsmelling savour."

Date:

Daily Thoughts and Reflections

_____

_____

Gratefulness and Praise

_____

_____

My Prayer

_____

_____

Love eternal we give unto you, God, for all that you have done for us.

shelter   *victory*

mercy   *healing*

forgiveness   *Holy Spirit*

compassion   *anointed*

abundant life   *prosperity*

salvation   *revelation*

eternal life   *courage*

Ephesians 5:19: "Speaking to yourselves in psalms and hymns and spiritual songs, singing and making melody in your heart to the Lord."

Date:

Daily Thoughts and Reflections

_____

_____

Gratefulness and Praise

_____

_____

My Prayer

_____

_____

Oh, the perfect path of life you have shown to your children. We will rejoice and sing unto you, O Lord.

Ephesians 5:20: "Giving thanks always for all things unto God and the Father in the name of our Lord Jesus Christ."

Date:

Daily Thoughts and Reflections

_____

_____

Gratefulness and Praise

_____

_____

My Prayer

_____

_____

We thank you, God, with grateful hearts, for who you are in our lives, giving us blessings from your hands.

Ephesians 6:1: "Children, obey your parents in the Lord: for this is right."

Date:

Daily Thoughts and Reflections

_____

_____

Gratefulness and Praise

_____

_____

My Prayer

_____

_____

We love and obey our parents unconditionally, God. And for this we are blessed beyond measure.

Ephesians 6:2–3: "Honour thy father and mother; which is the first commandment with promise; That it may be well with thee, and thou mayest live long on the earth."

Date:

Daily Thoughts and Reflections

_____

_____

Gratefulness and Praise

_____

_____

My Prayer

_____

_____

For beautiful blessings come from you, God, and your promises give us great hope for our future.

Philippians 1:10: "That ye may approve things that are excellent; that ye may be sincere and without offence till the day of Christ."

Date:

Daily Thoughts and Reflections

_____

_____

Gratefulness and Praise

_____

_____

My Prayer

_____

_____

Your ways, God, are highways, and your promises unfold and bless us greatly.

Philippians 2:10: "That at the name of Jesus every knee should bow, of things in heaven, and things in earth, and things under the earth."

Date:

Daily Thoughts and Reflections

_____

_____

Gratefulness and Praise

_____

_____

My Prayer

_____

_____

We humbly bend our knees and worship you, Jesus, for you are highly exalted and glorified above all creation.

Philippians 2:11: "And that every tongue should confess that Jesus Christ is Lord, to the glory of God the Father."

Date:

Daily Thoughts and Reflections

_____

_____

Gratefulness and Praise

_____

_____

My Prayer

_____

_____

Our tongues rejoice and confess that you are the Lord of our lives, Jesus.

❧

Philippians 2:13: "For it is God which worketh in you both to will and to do of his good pleasure."

Date:

Daily Thoughts and Reflections

_____

_____

Gratefulness and Praise

_____

_____

My Prayer

_____

_____

God propels us to our destiny, for he works mightily in us. This excites our spirit, for we love and desire to do his will.

Philippians 2:16: "Holding forth the word of life; that I may rejoice in the day of Christ, that I have not run in vain, neither laboured in vain."

Date:

Daily Thoughts and Reflections

_____

_____

Gratefulness and Praise

_____

_____

My Prayer

_____

_____

His promises to his beloved children are true, and on his word we can stand.

Philippians 4:4: "Rejoice in the Lord always: and again I say, Rejoice."

Date:

Daily Thoughts and Reflections

_____

_____

Gratefulness and Praise

_____

_____

My Prayer

_____

_____

It is good to rejoice in you, Lord, for you are the giver of life and have made us glad.

Philippians 4:6: "Be careful for nothing; but in every thing by prayer and supplication with thanksgiving let your requests be made known unto God."

Date:

Daily Thoughts and Reflections

_____

_____

Gratefulness and Prayer

_____

_____

My Prayer

_____

_____

We come to you with thankful hearts, God, for we know you hear us, your children, when we pray.

Philippians 4:7: "And the peace of God, which passeth all understanding, shall keep your hearts and minds through Christ Jesus."

Date:

Daily Thoughts and Reflections

_____

_____

Gratefulness and Praise

_____

_____

My Prayer

_____

_____

Thank you for your incredible peace, for my meditation is on you, sweet Jesus.

Philippians 4:8: "Finally, brethren, whatsoever things are true, whatsoever things are honest, whatsoever things are just, whatsoever things are pure, whatsoever things are lovely, whatsoever things are of good report; if there be any virtue, and if there be any praise, think on these things."

Date:

Daily Thoughts and Reflections

_____

_____

Gratefulness and Praise

_____

_____

My Prayer

_____

_____

Yes, God, I wholeheartedly delight my soul in you, for you have brightened my countenance and your glory is upon me.

❧

Philippians 4:9: "Those things, which ye have both learned, and received, and heard, and seen in me, do: and the God of peace shall be with you."

Date:

Daily Thoughts and Reflections

_____

_____

Gratefulness and Praise

_____

_____

My Prayer

_____

_____

I love your ways, God. They are planted deeply in my heart, and my soul has peace.

Philippians 4:13: "I can do all things through Christ which strengtheneth me."

Date:

Daily Thoughts and Reflections

_____

_____

Gratefulness and Praise

_____

_____

My Prayer

_____

_____

Absolutely nothing is impossible with you, God, for you work mightily in my life.

❧

Philippians 4: 19: "But my God shall supply all your need according to his riches in glory by Christ Jesus."

Date:

Daily Thoughts and Reflections

_____

_____

Gratefulness and Praise

_____

_____

My Prayer

_____

_____

God, your wonderful provisions fill our lives with your goodness, for you care for your children.

Colossians 1:27: "To whom God would make known what is the riches of the glory of this mystery among the Gentiles; which is Christ in you, the hope of glory."

Date:

Daily Thoughts and Reflections

_____

_____

Gratefulness and Praise

_____

_____

My Prayer

_____

_____

Jesus, thank you for living inside me. You have given me glorious hope and made me complete in your love.

Colossians 3:12: "Put on therefore, as the elect of God, holy and beloved, bowels of mercy, kindness, humbleness of mind, meekness, longsuffering."

Date:

Daily Thoughts and Reflections

_____

_____

Gratefulness and Praise

_____

_____

My Prayer

_____

_____

Let us be clothed with all his royalty, for he is our loving heavenly Father.

Colossians 3:13: "Forbearing one another, and forgiving one another, if any man quarrel against any: even as Christ forgave you, so also do ye."

Date:

Daily Thoughts and Reflections

_____

_____

Gratefulness and Praise

_____

_____

My Prayer

_____

_____

Let us always expect the very best from each other and build one another up in the Lord.

Colossians 3:14: "And above all these things put on charity, which is the bond of perfectness."

Date:

Daily Thoughts and Reflections

_____

_____

Gratefulness and Praise

_____

_____

My Prayer

_____

_____

It is with extreme joy we give from our hearts full of compassion for the needs of God's children.

Colossians 3:21: "Fathers, provoke not your children to anger, lest they be discouraged."

Date:

Daily Thoughts and Reflections

_____

_____

Gratefulness and Praise

_____

_____

My Prayer

_____

_____

Let us lovingly guide our precious children in all the ways of the Lord.

Colossians 3:23–24: "And whatsoever ye do, do it heartily, as to the Lord, and not unto men; Knowing that of the Lord ye shall receive the reward of inheritance: for ye serve the Lord Christ."

Date:

Daily Thoughts and Reflections

_____

_____

Gratefulness and Praise

_____

_____

My Prayer

_____

_____

We are lifted up and out of a world of mediocrity to live a life of excellence before the Lord, setting an example for all people.

2 Timothy 1:7: "For God hath not given us the spirit of fear; but of power, and of love, and of sound mind."

Date:

Daily Thoughts and Reflections

_____

_____

Gratefulness and Praise

_____

_____

My Prayer

_____

_____

We are well equipped for victory in all situations, for our great and awesome God goes before us, defeating our enemies.

Month Nine

Date:

Precious photos of my baby and me at month nine

Beautiful photos place here

Daily Thoughts and Reflections

_____

_____

Gratefulness and Praise

_____

_____

My Prayer

_____

_____

2 Timothy 3:15: "And that from a child thou hast known the holy scriptures, which are able to make thee wise unto salvation through faith which is in Christ Jesus."

Date:

Answered Prayer

_____

_____

Gratefulness and Praise

_____

_____

My Prayer

_____

_____

Thank you, God, for your word and for sending your son, Jesus, to save us, that we may have eternal life.

2 Timothy 3:16: "All scripture is given by inspiration of God, and is profitable for doctrine, for reproof, for correction, for instruction in righteousness."

Date:

Beautiful photos place here

Celebrations and Special Events

_____

_____

Gratefulness and Praise

_____

_____

My Prayer

_____

_____

All your words, God, are filled with wisdom, blessing our lives.

2 Timothy 3:17: "That a man of God may be perfect, thoroughly furnished unto all good works."

Date:

Daily Thoughts and Reflections

_____

_____

Gratefulness and Praise

_____

_____

My Prayer

_____

_____

We behold your beautiful words to us, and we are encouraged to share the good news.

Hebrews 4:12: "For the word of God is quick, and powerful, and sharper than any twoedged sword, piercing even to the dividing asunder of soul and spirit, and of the joints and marrow, and is a discerner of the thoughts and intents of the heart."

Date:

Daily Thoughts and Reflections

_____

_____

Gratefulness and Praise

_____

_____

My Prayer

_____

_____

O awesome God, we need you to mend our broken lives; you are the restorer of our hearts.

Hebrews 4:14 "Seeing then that we have a great high priest, that is passed into the heavens, Jesus the Son of God, let us hold fast our profession."

Date:

Daily Thoughts and Reflections

_____

_____

Gratefulness and Praise

_____

_____

My Prayer

_____

_____

Jesus, we praise you. Glory in the highest, for you have risen that we would be saved.

Hebrews 4:16: "Let us therefore come boldly unto the throne of grace, that we may obtain mercy, and find grace to help in time of need."

Date:

Daily Thoughts and Reflections

_____

_____

Gratefulness and Praise

_____

_____

My Prayer

_____

_____

We praise you, God, for you have provided your wonderful mercy and grace for our lives.

Hebrews 11:1: "Now faith is the substance of things hoped for, the evidence of things not seen."

Date:

Daily Thoughts and Reflections

_____

_____

Gratefulness and Praise

_____

_____

My Prayer

_____

_____

God, your wonderful gift of faith is tangible in our lives, and we are supernaturally enabled by your Holy Spirit to accomplish great things for your kingdom.

❧

Hebrews 11:11: "Through faith also Sarah herself received strength to conceive seed, and was delivered of a child when she was past age, because she judged him faithful who had promised."

Date:

Daily Thoughts and Reflections

_____

_____

Gratefulness and Praise

_____

_____

My Prayer

_____

_____

In faith we rely on our God and put our hope in him alone, for he is our deliverer.

Hebrews 12:1: "Wherefore seeing we also are compassed about with so great a cloud of witnesses, let us lay aside every weight, and the sin with doth so easily beset us, and let us run with patience the race that is set before us."

Date:

Daily Thoughts and Reflections

_____

_____

Gratefulness and Praise

_____

_____

My Prayer

_____

_____

God, your ministering holy angels change the very atmosphere of our lives and impart to us everything that heaven has to offer, as a marvelous blessing from you.

Hebrews 12:2: "Looking unto Jesus the author and finisher of our faith; who for the joy that was set before him endured the cross, despising the shame, and is set down at the right hand of the throne of God."

Date:

Daily Thoughts and Reflections

_____

_____

Gratefulness and Praise

_____

_____

My Prayer

_____

_____

You have done it all for us, the ones you love, Jesus. We glorify and praise your holy name, O Lamb of God.

Hebrews 12:28–29: "Wherefore we receiving a kingdom which cannot be moved, let us have grace, whereby we may serve God acceptably with reverence and godly fear: For our God is a consuming fire."

Date:

Daily Thoughts and Reflections

_____

_____

Gratefulness and Praise

_____

_____

My Prayer

_____

_____

You are the flame that burns in our hearts, God, and we love to do your will as your good children. Your will is our joyous pleasure forever.

Hebrews 13:19: "But I beseech you the rather to do this, that I may be restored to you the sooner."

Date:

Daily Thoughts and Reflections

_____

_____

Gratefulness and Praise

_____

_____

My Prayer

_____

_____

We eagerly expect you coming again soon, Jesus, O mighty savior and risen king.

Hebrews 13:20: "Now the God of peace, that brought again from the dead our Lord Jesus, that great shepherd of the sheep, through the blood of the everlasting covenant."

Date:

Daily Thoughts and Reflections

_____

_____

Gratefulness and Praise

_____

_____

My Prayer

_____

_____

You sacrificed your body and spilled your blood on the cross for our sins, so that we would be redeemed to eternal life.

Hebrews 13:21: "Make you perfect in every good work to do his will, working in you that which is well pleasing in his sight, through Jesus Christ; to whom be glory for ever and ever. Amen."

Date:

Daily Thoughts and Reflections

_____

_____

Gratefulness and Praise

_____

_____

My Prayer

_____

_____

You've enlivened my heart, God, and refined and shaped my life until it is purer than costly stones. Your glory is manifest on my life.

shelter

mercy

forgiveness

compassion

abundant life

salvation

eternal life

victory

healing

Holy Spirit

anointed

prosperity

revelation

courage

James 1:3: "Knowing this, that the trying of your faith worketh patience."

Date:

Daily Thoughts and Reflections

_____

_____

Gratefulness and Praise

_____

_____

My Prayer

_____

_____

We are tested to be sure, but let us keep our focus on the word of God, gaining insight and revelation as a blessing in our lives.

James 1:4: "But let patience have her perfect work, that ye may be perfect and entire, wanting nothing."

Date:

Daily Thoughts and Reflections

_____

_____

Gratefulness and Praise

_____

_____

My Prayer

_____

_____

Good things come from you, God. I surrender my life to you, for you reward generously.

James 1:5: "If any of you lack wisdom, let him ask of God, that giveth to all men liberally, and upbraideth not; and it shall be given him."

Date:

Daily Thoughts and Reflections

_____

_____

Gratefulness and Praise

_____

_____

My Prayer

_____

_____

We worship and adore you, God, for you reveal your wisdom to your children when we pray.

James 1:6: "But let him ask in faith, nothing wavering, For he that wavereth is like a wave of the sea driven with the wind and tossed."

Date:

Daily Thoughts and Reflections

_____

_____

Gratefulness and Praise

_____

_____

My Prayer

_____

_____

We are assured that when we ask, you generously give. We have anchored our faith in you, God.

James 1:17: "Every good gift and every perfect gift is from above, and cometh down from the Father of lights, with whom is no variable, neither shadow of turning."

Date:

Daily Thoughts and Reflections

_____

_____

Gratefulness and Praise

_____

_____

My Prayer

_____

_____

With grateful and exuberantly joyous hearts, we yield our lives to you, receiving all your wonderful blessings, Father God.

James 1:21: "Wherefore lay apart all filthiness and superfluity of naughtiness, and receive with meekness the engrafted word, which is able to save your souls."

Date:

Daily Thoughts and Reflections

_____

_____

Gratefulness and Praise

_____

_____

My Prayer

_____

_____

We rejoice in speaking words of life, for they are like a beautiful fragrance edifying and healing the soul.

James 1:25: "But whoso looketh into the perfect law of liberty, and continueth therein, he being not a forgetful hearer, but a doer of the work, this man shall be blessed in his deed."

Date:

Daily Thoughts and Reflections

_____
_____

Gratefulness and Praise

_____
_____

My Prayer

_____
_____

We will harvest abundant blessings, for we love your will. It brings a song of joy to our mouths.

James 2:5: "Hearken, my beloved brethren, Hath not God chosen the poor of this world rich in faith, and heirs of the kingdom which he hath promised to them that love him?"

Date:

Daily Thoughts and Reflections

_____
_____

Gratefulness and Praise

_____
_____

My Prayer

_____
_____

God's heart beats in one accord with his precious children, for they look to him as their only hope.

James 2:8: "If ye fulfil the royal law according to the scripture, Thou shalt love thy neighbour as thyself, ye do well."

Date:

Daily Thoughts and Reflections

_____

_____

Gratefulness and Praise

_____

_____

My Prayer

_____

_____

It will go well with us; a hedge of protection and God's love will cover our family.

James 2:18: "Yea, a man may say, Thou hast faith, and I have works: show me thy faith without thy works, and I will show thee my faith by my works."

Date:

Daily Thoughts and Reflections

_____

_____

Gratefulness and Praise

_____

_____

My Prayer

_____

_____

With the power of your Holy Spirit supernaturally working in our lives, we will accomplish your will for us, paving the way for our children and generations to come. With exuberant joy and passion we run to accomplish the mission and the vision you have given us, leaving a legacy.

James 2:23: "And the scripture was fulfilled which saith, Abraham believed God, and it was imputed unto him for righteousness: and he was called the Friend of God."

Date:

Daily Thoughts and Reflections

_____

_____

Gratefulness and Praise

_____

_____

My Prayer

_____

_____

We are blessed with your friendship, for we draw near to you, God.

James 3:17: "But the wisdom that is from above is first pure, then peaceable, gentle, and easy to be entreated, full of mercy and good fruits, without partiality, and without hypocrisy."

Date:

Daily Thoughts and Reflections

_____

_____

Gratefulness and Praise

_____

_____

My Prayer

_____

_____

We love you, God, for you make our lives flourish with your goodness.

James 3:18: "And the fruit of righteousness is sown in peace of them that make peace."

Date:

Daily Thoughts and Reflections

_____

_____

Gratefulness and Praise

_____

_____

My Prayer

_____

_____

O God, with words of life we sow your peace into all hearts.

James 4:6: "But he giveth more grace. Wherefore he saith, God resisteth the proud, but giveth grace unto the humble."

Date:

Daily Thoughts and Reflections

_____

_____

Gratefulness and Praise

_____

_____

My Prayer

_____

_____

You are lovely to behold, God, for your grace flows in abundance into my life.

James 5:13: "Is any among you afflicted? Let him pray. Is any merry? Let him sing psalms."

Date:

Daily Thoughts and Reflections

_____

_____

Gratefulness and Praise

_____

_____

My Prayer

_____

_____

You soothe our souls, God, and make our hearts rejoice. We will sing of your love for us.

❦

James 5:16: "Confess your faults one to another, and pray one for another, that ye may be healed. The effectual fervent prayer of a righteous man availeth much."

Date:

Daily Thoughts and Reflections

_____

_____

Gratefulness and Praise

_____

_____

My Prayer

_____

_____

We humble ourselves before you, God, letting go of past sins and praying for the needs of others.

James 5:17: "Elias was a man subject to like passions as we are, and he prayed earnestly that it might not rain: and it rained not on the earth by the space of three years and six months."

Date:

Daily Thoughts and Reflections

_____

_____

Gratefulness and Praise

_____

_____

My Prayer

_____

_____

God's wonderworking power in our lives is able to move mountains when we pray.

James 5:18: "And he prayed again, and the heaven gave rain, and the earth brought forth her fruit."

Date:

Daily Thoughts and Reflections

_____

_____

Gratefulness and Praise

_____

_____

My Prayer

_____

_____

As we come before you, God, with sincere hearts, you hear our prayers.

I Peter I:3: "Blessed be the God and Father of our Lord Jesus Christ, which according to his abundant mercy hath begotten us again unto a lively hope by the resurrection of Jesus Christ from the dead."

Date:

Daily Thoughts and Reflections

_____

_____

Gratefulness and Praise

_____

_____

My Prayer

_____

_____

Our love for you, God, is wondrous, for we are filled with joyous hope and eternal life through your son, Jesus Christ.

Joy! , joy! , joy! Incredible joy! My baby's birth and the wonderful experiences of this beautiful day!
"O Happy day God's miracle to me!"

Date:

Precious photos of my baby and me at month nine

Beautiful photos place here

Daily Thoughts and Reflections

_____

_____

Gratefulness and Praise

_____

_____

My Prayer

_____

_____

Psalm 18:19: "He brought me forth also into a large place; he delivered me, because he delighted in me."

Our first embrace and the wonderful experiences of this beautiful day:

Date:

Beautiful photos place here

_____

_____

_____

_____

_____

_____

_____

Our happy new family and the wonderful experiences of this beautiful day

Date:

Beautiful photos place here

Our journey home and the wonderful experiences of this beautiful day:

Date:

Beautiful photos place here

left margin (top to bottom): shelter   mercy   forgiveness   compassion   abundant life   salvation   eternal life

right margin (top to bottom): victory   healing   Holy Spirit   anointed   prosperity   revelation   courage

Love joy peace hope faith grace favour

victory

healing

Holy Spirit

anointed

prosperity

revelation

courage

Look at my baby grow!

shelter

mercy

forgiveness

compassion

abundant life

salvation

eternal life

My baby's first handprints and the wonderful experiences of this beautiful day:

Date:

Cute handprints and beautiful photos place here

My baby's first footprints and the wonderful experiences of this beautiful day:

Date:

Cute footprints and beautiful photos place here

shelter
mercy
forgiveness
compassion
abundant life
salvation
eternal life

victory
healing
Holy Spirit
anointed
prosperity
revelation
courage

Celebration of my baby shower and the wonderful experiences of this beautiful day:

Date:

Beautiful photos place here

My baby's first noises, gestures, laughter, words and the wonderful experiences of this beautiful day:

Date:

Beautiful photos place here

My baby's first time crawling and the wonderful experiences of this beautiful day:

Date:

Beautiful photos place here

Love joy peace hope faith grace favour

My baby's first time eating and tasting food, and the wonderful experiences of this beautiful day:

Date:

Beautiful photos place here

_____

_____

_____

_____

_____

_____

_____

God's presence   blessings   229   righteousness   protection

My baby's first steps walking and the wonderful experiences of this beautiful day:

Date:

Beautiful photos place here

shelter   *mercy*   *forgiveness*   *compassion*   *abundant life*   *salvation*   *eternal life*

victory   *healing*   *Holy Spirit*   *anointed*   *prosperity*   *revelation*   *courage*

My baby's first time sleeping in crib and the wonderful experiences of this beautiful day:

Date:

Beautiful photos place here

_____

_____

_____

_____

_____

_____

_____

_____

My baby's first shoes& slippers and the wonderful experiences of this beautiful day:

Date:

Beautiful photos place here

victory

healing

Holy Spirit

anointed

prosperity

revelation

courage

shelter

mercy

forgiveness

compassion

abundant life

salvation

eternal life

My baby's first pajamas & outfits and the wonderful experiences of this beautiful day:

Date:

Beautiful photos place here

shelter

mercy

forgiveness

compassion

abundant life

salvation

eternal life

victory

healing

Holy Spirit

anointed

prosperity

revelation

courage

_____
_____
_____
_____
_____
_____
_____

My baby's first haircut and the wonderful experiences of this beautiful day:

Date:

Beautiful photos place here

_____

_____

_____

_____

_____

_____

_____

My baby's dedication and the wonderful experiences of this beautiful day

Date:

Beautiful photos place here

I Peter I:4: "To an inheritance incorruptible, and undefiled, and that fadeth not away, reserved in heaven for you."

Date:

Answered Prayer

_____

_____

Gratefulness and Praise

_____

_____

My Prayer

_____

_____

Our deeply rooted faith promises us life eternal and that we will live forever with our God. Hallelujah!

I Peter 1:5: "Who are kept by the power of God through faith unto salvation ready to be revealed in the last time."

Date:

Beautiful photos place here

Celebrations and Special Events

_____

_____

Gratefulness and Praise

_____

_____

My Prayer

_____

_____

You embrace me, God, with your love for me as your precious child.

Acknowledgements

Authors Frank and Janet Cseke with the guidance and help of our two loving daughters.

And our Lord and Savior Jesus Christ

Beautiful One
A Gift Within